Ti

Algorithms

$10,000/Month Business Plan Using Your Personal TikTok Account | Learn How to Make Money Online Right Now from Home, building a Brand and Become an Influencer

By

Leonard Carli & MarketingLegacy

The information in the following pages is broadly considered a truthful and accurate account of facts and as such, any inattention, use, or misuse of the information in question by the reader will render any resulting actions solely under their purview. There are no scenarios in which the publisher or the original author of this work can be in any fashion deemed liable for any hardship or damages that may befall them after undertaking information described herein.

Additionally, the information in the following pages is intended only for informational purposes and should thus be thought of as universal. As befitting its nature, it is presented without assurance regarding its prolonged validity or interim quality. Trademarks that are mentioned are done without written consent and can in no way be considered an endorsement from the trademark holder.

Table of Content

Introduction

This book is about "TikTok Tips." The book seeks to establish how to get famous on TikTok: a guide for beginners to get more likes and views on your TikTok videos. As the role of social media expands in societal life, it also poses a substantial platform for value creation in a business sense. This book explores this subject with the aim of providing crucial tips, skills, and business acumen required to make TikTok not only an exciting opportunity but a valuable one as well.

Also, don't forget as more and more of the world gets in social media, more and more people will expect to be able to find their favorite businesses and brands online. They want to communicate with you, to know about their product, and they want to know that you care. Making your customers feel connected to you will help your profits go up because they will feel connected to the product they are buying.

Getting into social media marketing can be tough and overwhelming. It can feel like a huge, giant project, and often business owners, because of this feeling, decide that it's not worth it. But it is. It is 100 percent worth it as you will be able to interact with prospective clients more easily and find out exactly what they are searching for.

Digital marketing methods are also much cheaper compared to traditional marketing means, which enables you to reach a much larger audience at very low costs. You also get to track responses to your marketing efforts, which in essence enables you to find out what is working and what you can improve on.

Helps your brand: As you know, your brand is the most valuable thing in your business. Every business is fighting to increase or maintain the visibility of their brand. With a strong brand, you have the edge over your competition. Customers are drawn and tend to be more loyal to popular brands. With social media, you have an affordable digital marketing method for syndicating content and increasing your business' visibility.

You first come up with a great strategy for social media and engage with a wide audience of potential customers. The social media profiles for your business need to be complete and optimized in order to attract your targeted audience. The best way to increase brand awareness is by generating content. You must publish posts on the regular and invite people to engage with your content. The "likes" and "shares" will introduce your business to new audiences who will potentially become your customers. The following are some things you can expect social media to do to help you increase brand awareness.

Help you to create visual content: People are more likely to share content that has an image as opposed to text only. So, ensure that you put high-quality images in your content.

Showcase your personality: it's important to let your charisma shine through. If you deliver the message in a fun and personable way, people subconsciously drop their guards, and it endears your business to them.

Marketing pays real dividends: Marketing is viewed largely as an expense even though in essence it is an investment. It is a crucial activity, especially when it comes to attracting the attention of new customers and prospective clients. You are able to develop services, and products demand and eventually turn prospective customers into actual customers. Expanding your social media marketing channels means having a presence in as many media platforms as possible.

Improve search engine visibility: Every business wants to be able to increase the amount of user engagement and traffic that they have. But is it really possible to do all of this if your potential customers aren't even able to find you when they go online? There are a number of ways that you are able to increase the potential customers to your site, but having a good social media profile can help you dominate those first search result pages naturally and organically, and this in turn, increases the profits that you earn.

When you are thinking about this, you can consider the fact that millennials already spend a ton of time on social platforms, and having your own is going to increase the value of your company more than ever. It cannot only help you to generate more business and profits for yourself, but it can also stop some of the brand negativity it takes to reach top positions.

It acts as the mouthpiece for your company: Whether you have been in the industry for a long time, or you are just starting, having a positive word of mouth for your business will help you to gain more customers and keep your business running. Social media marketing can be a great way to help you as a business owner interact with your customers and generate positive buzz via word of mouth. You can use it to talk about policies in the company, team activities, new launches, and any other information that is needed for the business.

Essential social media marketing plan campaign tools

While a successful social media marketing campaign can bring with it a wide variety of potential benefits, it can only do so if you go into it with the right tools from the start.

A good plan: One of the things that you really need to have is a plan that will support your brand and efforts for many years to come. Such a plan will keep you on track and help you to achieve your marketing ambitions. The plan does not need to be as elaborate as a scientific manual. However, it should be clearly written with a well-defined path and exact steps that need to be taken in order to achieve your business's overall aim. If this plan and strategy are then communicated to your team, then your whole business will soon start reaping the dividends of your extensive and elaborate plans. Likewise, if you are working all alone then having clearly defined goals will make it much more likely that you actually reach them.

An excellent product or service: Any social media marketing or advertising campaigns will not bear fruit if you do not have an excellent product or service to offer your future customers. Excellent products or services are those that solve a problem your customers have while at the same time providing a lasting solution. To achieve this, you will need to listen to your customers and consider their opinions.

A presentable brand: Having a professional brand is absolutely essential for your success. A brand is much more than just your company's logo. It entails a lot more including what people get to hear and talk about as well as what they feel and think about your business. Make sure that you put together a budget that will support your efforts in building a powerful brand that will stand out from the crowd.

An excellent pitch: As a business owner, you can expect numerous individuals to ask you over and over again about your business and your products. You need to be ready with quality, interesting answers that will intrigue them. Avoid making the mistake of replying with long, boring answers that will drive your potential customers away. Prepare a pitch and make it interesting, fun, and exciting. Then make sure that you are able to deliver it anytime anyone asks about your business regardless of what online setting you find yourself in

Understand ROI: One of the biggest misconceptions that many business leaders will have about Return on Investment (ROI) is that it pertains to revenue-generating actions. Unfortunately, this is far from the truth. ROI pertains mostly to the brand-building methods that are more profitable in the long run than the conversion of actual sales due to the ad campaign. Social media is about the process of building customer conversation and connectivity. It is about using social media outlets to reach those that are not familiar with your brand and helping them to understand your passions as a company.

There are a few metrics that need to be monitored to examine the impact your social media account is having on your ROI. These include:

- Lifetime Value

- Churn

- The overall cost of operation

Lifetime value is a measurement that will calculate the frequency as well as the annual total of purchases for each customer prior to the ad campaign and after the ad campaign. By using the lifetime value as a calculative measure for the ROI you are setting a baseline for the impact that the social media ad campaign is having on your bottom line.

To understand how social media is hurting or improving your customers' loyalty, you can check the churn. The churn will tell you how many customers you have gained or lost, as well as the volume by which it went up or down. Next, you will work towards understanding the concept that a dollar that is saved is also a dollar that is earned. It can be quite difficult to measure the ROI of your social media account; however, you can measure the social media's impact that has taken place on the brand's equity, as well as the benefit of the bottom line.

2020 Trends

Social media is here to stay, and it looks like it is only going to become even more influential as it continues to evolve and change quickly to keep up with the ever-growing demands of society. Experiences will only become more interactive, immersive, and influential, and for a business to survive, it must be leveraging the social media experience at every opportunity. Social media marketing is here to stay.

Innovation in marketing in this era is essential. As a business owner, you need to keep yourself updated with some of the latest trends in marketing and advertising. There are quite a number of innovations that will be adapted in 2019 that will help to take your business to the next level. For the foreseeable future at least, especially these are a few important trends to keep tabs on, including the increasing importance of influencers, VR and AR, sales enablement, artificial intelligence, and even more personalized content.

Influencers will be more important than ever

Come the year 2020, influencer marketing is projected to become an industry capable of raking in 10 billion dollars. Given the rise of influencers across every social media platform channel, this is a very real possibility. Gen Z and the millennials have also embraced influencers in their lives, welcoming the power of their social media storytelling, even using that power to help them make decisions on whether they should purchase a product or service. Watching unboxing videos or product reviews on YouTube, where an influencer shows off the latest gadget, beauty product, fashion haul, etc., has created a unique and immersive experience.

The following are some of the reasons why marketers are turning to influencers to promote their products:

Influencers have earned their followers' trust: someone is more likely to buy a product when it's recommended by a person that they trust. An influencer has already earned the trust of their followers, and it puts them in a better position to recommend products.

Influencers give you access to a targeted audience: promoting a product to a small niche-audience is much more rewarding than blasting an ad to a crowd who couldn't care less about your product. When you use an influencer, you gain access to a laser-targeted audience who are likely to purchase your product.

Relatively inexpensive: influencers are very affordable as long as you don't go for Hollywood stars and athletes. For instance, micro-influencers charge between $200 and $250 for a post, which is a reasonable price considering they are exposing you to thousands of their targeted followers. Some marketers seem to be of the notion that influencers are too expensive when it isn't the case at all.

Boosts SEO: another method of getting strong backlinks to your site is by leveraging social media influencers. When influencers link to your site, it boosts both your domain authority and page authority, which in turn improves SEO.

While it seems as though influencers hit the mainstream relatively recently, it is already an established part of the status quo to the point that well-known influencers are already making thousands of dollars, if not more, for sponsorships and brand associations. As such, if you have already heard of an influencer, then odds are you likely can't afford them if you are just starting out. This is where the latest tier of influencers, known as micro-influencers come into play.

Micro-influencers, as the name implies, do not have followers in the millions, or even in the hundreds of thousands, instead, they typically have around 50,000 followers or less. While the numbers may not be as high, the followers these micro-influencers have tend to be far more committed than their larger peers, to the point a food brand would see a better ROI working with a food blogger with 50,000 followers and a reasonable budget than a famous alternative which the price is 10 times as high.

The trend of drilling down to find even smaller and more dedicated followings is only going to increase in 2019 to the point where nano-influencers, those with a max of 10,000 dedicated followers, are going to start becoming relevant as well. Those who are members of these smaller communities tend to be the most dedicated at all, which means that if their favorite nano-influencer recommends your brand, the conversion rate is typically greater than 50 percent. As these individuals can often be bought for $100 or some free merchandise, the ROI on this type of social media marketing is only going to continue to increase.

What's more, many of these individuals are completely new to the business, which means that they are anxious to form long-term partnerships. As they don't require a large budget to work with, you may be in a place to easily lock an individual down early if you find someone that is clearly going to a big hit once they become a bit more well-known.

Chapter 1: Get Famous

Common Mistakes in Tiktok

When you get on TikTok, it is important that you understand that your success is not guaranteed just because you created an account and shared a few posts. When it comes to TikTok, many businesses are trying to reach the same audience as you are, so you need to make sure that you stand out in the crowd. The market is far from being "tapped out," but if you come onto a platform without knowing how to use it effectively, you are quickly going to get overlooked as your audience favors brands that come in with a strategy.

Here, you are going to learn what risks to avoid when using TikTok, in general, to ensure that you are not wasting your time using the wrong growth strategies online. You will learn what mistakes to avoid on each specific platform later, but for now, it is important that you understand the general risks to avoid so that you can have a massive impact online from day one.

Overstretching Yourself

Every single TikTok platform comes with a learning curve that you will need to endure in order to discover to master the platform and begin earning a high return on your TikTok marketing efforts. Regardless of whether or not you have already been on the platform, if you are not yet used to using that platform for marketing, you will need to learn how to adjust your approach and ensure that it is optimized for marketing so that you can increase your earnings. When you are looking to use TikTok for marketing, it is important that you do not overstretch yourself as this can lead to not having the required attention to enduring each learning curve and actually put that platform to use.

In order to ensure that you are not overstretching yourself, start by being honest about how much time you have each day to master your TikTok. If you only have a small amount of time per day or a few hours per week, it may be ideal to start out on the platform that is most likely to earn you an income. Then grow from there so that you are giving yourself enough time to understand each platform thoroughly. Once you have understood that first platform, then you can go ahead and start branching out to others so that you can master those as well.

Although you may want to grow big online quickly, it is important to understand where the balance lies when it comes to your growth. That is, it is a lot more productive to go big on one platform at a time than it is to spread yourself so thin that none of your platforms gain traction and you miss the mark on every TikTok site you try. You will find that you master each platform and grow a lot more quickly this way, making it easier for you to start generating great success online relatively quickly.

Spending Time on the Wrong Platforms

Another big risk that you might make online is spending time on the wrong platforms or targeting the wrong parts of the platforms. If you are not directing your time and attention properly, you can quickly get drawn into taking actions that are not productive to your overall goal, which leaves you at risk of wasting a lot of time and not getting a lot of results.

Just because you may personally prefer one platform over another, or you may personally feel like one is better suited to your business compared to another, does not mean that this is actually the best choice. You need to go where your audience is and position yourself directly in front of them, or you are going to find yourself falling flat on your face online.

Not Embracing the Learning Curve

When people get on TikTok, one of the biggest disservices they can do for themselves and their business is to fail to embrace the learning curve that comes with being on TikTok for marketing purposes. If you get on TikTok and fail to embrace the learning curve or try to do everything your way, you are going to find rather quickly that this is ineffective and that you are going to struggle to succeed online. While you certainly do need to embrace authenticity and freedom of expression online, failing to understand the basic concepts of how to get seen and heard online will only result in you struggling to grow your business.

The learning curve can take a few days, a few weeks, or even a few months, depending on how much time you have to invest in TikTok and what you are doing to learn about the learning curve itself. If you want to accelerate this time, reading books like this one and paying attention to regular algorithm changes, new releases, and platform updates is a great opportunity to make sure that you are learning everything there is to know as quickly as possible. Aside from consuming the information, you also need to practice putting it to work online so that you can ensure that you are aware of both what the information is and how it works in practice. The more you read, learn, and integrate TikTok strategies online, the faster you will be at getting your business out there and for an online impact.

That being said, make sure that you are not going too quickly online, either. If you change your strategy too frequently, no matter what platform you are on, you will find yourself struggling to stay seen because people will grow confused with what it is that you are trying to achieve. You need to be willing to give each strategy the time required to allow it to accumulate reasonable results based on your efforts. So you can determine whether or not it worked, how it could have been improved, and what can be maintained when you start adjusting your strategies.

Blending Personal with Professional

Finally, even if you are running a personal brand, you need to be cautious about how much you blend your personal life with your professional life. Attempting to blend your personal and professional lives too much can result in your oversharing online and muddying the face of your business. You need to be cautious when it comes to building a brand, especially a personal one. You must ensure that you are not sharing information that could result in you taking away from the reputation or clarity of your business. In other words, even if you have a personal brand, keep your professional and personal lives separate to avoid having personal information leak into your business, and destroy your professionalism.

Even if you are well-meaning, there will be many parts of your personal life that are simply not on-brand and, if you share them, it could result in you being seen as confusing or unprofessional. At the end of the day, even if you are sharing a personal brand, there are certain parts of your life that people simply do not want to read about or heed. The people who are following you will be more interested in the stuff that relates to them, or problems they may be facing, over anything else. This is not because people do not care about you, but because you are positioning yourself and your personal brand as a business. You need to be prepared to behave like a business.

If you do want to have a personal online platform, make sure that you keep your personal accounts private and separate from your business accounts. You can always share your business life with your personal friends but refrain from sharing your personal life with your business connections, unless it in some way makes sense to your business. For example, if you are starting a fashion blog, you can share about fashion topics with your professional network but refrain from sharing about your love life or relationships unless it in some way can be tied into your outfit. If you were to wear a cute outfit on a date, for example, you could share this, but do not share about your hardships or troubles that your relationship may be facing online as this will only lead to you being seen as unprofessional. If you want to be seen as a professional business and have the opportunity to do business like a professional, you need to behave like a professional online at all times.

Chapter 2: Optimize Your Profile

1. Look at the for-you-page

The for-you-page on tik-tok is very important and can help you to come up with video ideas. So to use them for your page to come up with video ideas, just start scrolling through the for-you-page. As you're scrolling through the for-you-page, you're going to come across particular music like 3 to 5 times. If you do, then, that's a huge sign that if you create a video using that music, your video will blow up. So it's recommended that you use the music that appeared on the for-you-page several times. The for-you algorithm favors music that is currently gaining popularity. They favor video ideas too that are going viral, which you can say music that is trendy at that moment. So to become popular on tik-tok, all you've to do is to follow the trends and make your own version of the trends. The cool thing about the trends is that they operate like a tournament challenge, where everyone is trying to win the challenge. Everyone is fighting to win the battle of the trends. Therefore, you've to copy the trends that you see on the app if you want to have any challenge at succeeding at all on tik-tok. The only mistake that many content producers on the platform make is that they just literally copy the trends; this is a huge mistake to make. Don't copy the trends directly but instead make your own version of the trend. The trend is a popup idea that everyone is trying to steal and make his or her own version of it. It's just like the zoom challenge, some people were just literally copying other people, but the smart ones came up with their oven version of the challenge. You can take a trend and make it different by putting a different ending to your video to get many likes. TO stand out on this app, you've to be able to differentiate yourself from other people on the app too. You also have to be ready to risk and experiment.

2. Utilize Hashtags

The hashtag page is very important for you as a content creator on tik-tok. If you're new on the platform and you're trying to get noticed, then use the hash-tags in all your content. Also, if you're familiar with social media, then understanding the hash-tags on the tik-tok platform shouldn't be a problem for you. The hashtags on this platform are extremely important. Understand that tik-tok is still a relatively new social media platform. Tik-tok itself isn't more than 2 years old, and the earlier you jump on the tik-tok platform; the more hashtags are going to be relevant for you. The reason for this is that a lot of people are searching and using hashtags to find certain information on the platform. And it's going to remain more relevant just because of the way tik-tok is set up.

Hashtags are a huge part of navigating on tik-tok, so when you use hashtags. On tik-tok, they'll help you to get a following more than how Instagram does it. If you need help finding relevant hashtags to use on your videos, you can use a hashtags generator like Seekmetrics.com and then theallhastag.com. Keep in mind that there are no , relevant articles. Hashtags and trends are the most beneficial things that you can use when it comes to finding fans and followers on the tik-tok platform. Now the hashtags on tik-tok go hand in hand with trends because the trendy hashtags on the platform are often challenges and other things that are moving quickly.

Hashtags are the keys to getting on the for-you-page. You can use hashtags like #fyp, which stands for your page, to get on the for-you-page. Also use #Lfl, which stands for like-for-like. Use other hashtags like #foryoupage #foryou, #featuredme, another way to find hashtags to use is just to type in the hash key, and you'll see a whole lot of tags that a bunch of people has used. It's great to use a current hashtag because that will get you featured on the for-you-page. If you just type in a hashtag, you'll see a whole bunch of tags that already have a bunch of views. At the time of writing, The hashtag #transformUrDrom have about 4.2M views. The hashtag #rookiethings have about 888.6 views #that made my day 12.7 million views. #all brand new has about 504.2million views. #summer prince has about 22.7 views. try to use the top three tags and to give you a much bigger chance of getting on the for-you-page.

You can use tags that tell other people to follow you on tiktok. For instance, if you look at the hashtag #lfl or #l4l, #f4f (Follow for following) #fff, you'll see underage children liking post with those hashtags so that you will come and follow them too. So when you use those tags, all those kids to like your page, however, don't like theirs too, just persuade them to like yours.

So Use every single one of the hashtags in your videos. So what you should do is to look a the hashtag page all the time before you create any video. A brand new hashtag usually comes out each morning. Look at the descriptions of other people's videos and then film your own version of it. Nobody wants to see the same thing repeatedly. So add that flavor and twist to your content. If you make a great video that stands out using hashtags, you'll be noticed by tik-tok. If you want to make a video on skits, then go and find different hashtags on skits and use everyone on them. When someone clicks on any of your hashtags, they'll be able to see your videos, and they might follow you and like all of your videos. Hashtags are very important, especially if you're using songs in your videos. Always, a hashtag from the for-you-page. If you're creating a slow-motion video, then use slow hashtag motion and lip-sync. Basically, use a lot of hashtags that will go along with the video. Don't use hashtags that don't make sense with the video. Use many hashtags that are super relevant to the videos that you're making.

So you've to start utilizing hashtags. Use only three hashtags when creating your videos or when posting your videos. Now the reason why tik-tok only allows three hashtags it's because, hashtags are extremely on the platform. Unlike, Instagram that you can use up to 50 irrelevant hashtags, you can't use up to 50 hashtags on tik-tok. So don't use more than three hashtags on Tik-tok if you want your hashtags to be valuable on the platform.

3. Look differently in the video

Try as much as possible to change how your video looks like from other people's videos. You can choose to go outside when you film your videos. Use great lighting in every video. Also, try to change one thing in the video. For instance, if you're doing a rotation challenge video and everyone is doing it from their bedroom mirror, you can try to somewhere like forever 21 and use their mirror to film your video. Why drive to such a place, you may ask? It's because your lightning will stand out, and your background will also be super different from other videos. Also, if you're doing a lip challenge, you can try to spice

31

things up by doing something unexpected in the video, such as using two people in your video. If you're making a video for the wanna listen to trend, you can get your friends to join in the "wanna listen to challenge." Because your video has more than one person, your video will stand out, unlike other videos, which are shooting with only one person in the background. So if you want to get more likes on tik-tok, then the most important key is for you to stand out.

4. Keep your videos short

Let your videos be between the divisions of 6 to 15 seconds long. Although tik-tok allows you videos that are 60 seconds long, the videos that have found success on the platform are videos that are just 15 seconds long. Although there are videos that are up to 45 seconds long on the platform. 15 seconds Long video is the norm. Keep your video under 15 seconds. Nobody has the time to sit down and binge-watch long videos, they just want a video that they can watch before they scroll past the page. Therefore, shorter videos are definitely better than longer videos on this platform.

5. Create horizontal videos

Always MAKE sure that your videos are kept horizontal, avoid creating vertical videos or videos with black bars. Let your video fill the entire screen. Even if it fills up the entire screen, it's not enough reason for you to start filming sideways, always correctly film your videos. Most people are used to holding their videos, straight, and they don't want to keep turning their phones to the side just to watch your video. People are lazy these days, so take note. Also, the tik-tok algorithm favors videos that are filmed vertically.

6. Good light and good quality video is the bomb

The best way to make your videos look good is to use good lighting in your videos, in fact, that's one of the most important things that you've to consider when making tik-tok videos. Now, if you don't have a ring light sitting in your house, then a good way to get good lighting is to use natural lighting. Do your videos outside because slow-motion videos look a lot better when you do them outside. If you want to create a video that has good lighting, then film in a place that has a lot of lights. If you don't have artificial lights to use, then you can go outside and use your back camera. So as mentioned before, your videos to be super clear even if you are creating a video that in the darkness, it still needs to have a certain level of brightness. They are not a lot of bad quality videos that find success on this platform diagram where you can see mediocre quality kind of videos and on YouTube. You know platforms like YouTube are general sharing type of platforms, but on tiktok, people are mostly on the platform to get entertained any kind of poor quality video will easily turn them off.

7. Use Lip sync to create funny sounds

Don't just use the lip sync because you want to change your voice, instead use it because you want to give people something funny. Don't just do the lip sync on your bed, it won't be really funny. Try to pop things up. Go outside and put on some props. Put in the extra effort to make the lip sync look good.

8. Use a skit with no words in it

If you're using a skit make sure that the skit is something that anyone can understand, if you need to take out the words, then do that, so that the words that you're using in your video becomes a universal language. Tik-tok is a universal app; it's an app that brings the whole world together in one place, which means that people from all over the world are using the app now. so if there are no words in your video, then it will get a larger reach and hundreds of likes, because people from china, Ukraine, Africa, and all the non-speaking English countries will be able to watch your videos

9. Edit your videos off the app

Use a better video editing app like final cut and adobe premiere pro to edit your video. Tik-tok also has some great video editing features and special filters that you can use if the ideas that you're filming requires them. But if you've got a simple idea, then it's better that you edit off the app and upload the video from the camera roll. You don't even any fancy camera or gadget to film your video; all you need is your iPhone 8 . Form your iPhone camera; you can basically change the settings on your recording to produce higher quality and smoother looking videos. You don't even have to shoot your videos in 4k. If you're always trying to do the airdrops, then your video will take too long to shot, edit, and upload because the quality is high. The most recommended camera settings are 1080p and 60 fps. For simple editing, you can use an app like the final cut pro on a mac book. You can also use video stars on the iPhone. There is also a popular video editing app that a lot of people on tik-tok uses, you can use that as well. Literally, you can choose to use any video editing software that you feel very comfortable with. When you upload from the camera roll, make sure that you've got the music(that is if you

used a lip-synced music or a trendy one) favorite it, and replaced your original audio with the music that you found on tik-tok. So that way, you are making sure that the audio isn't messed up, and at the same time, you're giving the original artist credit, and you'll show up in a music folder.

If you don't take note, of this, then you'll forget to give the original artist credit for his song because you're in haste to publish your video on the app. if you take the time to give the original artist credit, you'll get seen by other people that used that music, and that will make more people see your video, click on it and follow you.

10. Engage with your fans

So this means treating others the same way that you want to be treated. Once you start getting a few fans, try to like every single person's comment. Just to appreciate your fans that are supporting you. So if you've a new account and the account is just beginning to grow, then start replying to other people's comments. If someone commented on your video, then reply that person back, like the person's comment, and like the person's videos too so that those people will keep coming back to your page to watch your video.

11. Show your fans love

Don't forget, the first day that you jumped for joy on your first 100 likes. Don't forget where you started because you are not going to be anything without your fans. Don't just do what you're doing to get more fans and likes, but keep in mind that you're creating stuff and putting it out to the world for everyone to see, so if you can make your videos a positive experience, for your fans. Spread love not to hate because there is already too much hate out there, and you don't want to be basically adding to the hate that is already out there.

12. Think about the type of content that you want to post

Before you make any content, always ask yourself if you're making the content for yourself or for other people? Ask yourself if you want to show people your talent (that is, you want other people to notice you), or you just want to make people laugh and entertained. So always, ask yourself those questions before creating any video.

13. Think about your audience

Your audience is really going to be a huge determining factor in the kind of content that you're going to create. Always think about your audience and figure out what your audience would like and go create that. If you've younger fans, then you might not want to create a video that has bad words in it. The reason is that for you to become famous on tik-tok or on any social media app, today, you've to become an influencer, meaning that you'll always have an influence on people good or bad, no matter what you're doing. SO always, think about what you're posting.

14. Don't make content that encourages negativity

You don't need to bully someone to be funny on the app. Don't go and make fun of someone that doesn't have an arm with the hashtag, "you wish you had this" on the app just to be funny. Or compare someone that is experiencing hair loss to an egg, just to be funny. This is not good at all. If someone is getting bullied over something that they have no power over, then that's confirmed bullying because the person cannot change that thing about his or her self. If you see any of such bullying, don't hesitate to report it. If you're afraid to speak up to the poster of the video, then you can use the report button on tik-tok to report that person's video for bullying and harassment. Those bullying videos are getting saturated these days on tik-tok, and of course, tik-tok usually frowns at such videos. The apps try it's best to hide negative content and foster positivity. They want to create a community that welcomes everyone, so when there's a situation that makes people sign out in the video, then it's they won't take it likely at all.

Chapter 3: Choose A Niche

At this point, you already know how to post on TikTok. You have also been able to come up with a great bio and a fantastic brand, and you start putting up random posts containing great content. You relax and expect the comments and the likes to come rolling in while your followers increase because you have done all that you need to do.

Unfortunately, you do not make the progress that you are expecting. It appears there are not a lot of people who are interested in the posts you put up. This is undoubtedly an issue. It, however, might be more related to the way you make your posts and not actually about what you post. There are lots of people who make use of TikTok for marketing. They can do this because they have an understanding of the way the platform operates and also know how to make use of it in ways that are beneficial to them and guarantee amazing results.

A lot of marketers can stand out from the crowd by selecting a particular niche and sticking to it. This way, they gain a reputation among users as the authority in these niches. Due to this, we will take the time to look into selecting a niche and staying unique on TikTok. Before we go on, it is essential to know what a niche is.

Definition of a Niche

We could spend the whole day talking about selecting the right niche. The truth, however, is that this would be futile if you have no idea what exactly a niche is.

A niche market is a smaller section under a bigger market. It can be likened to a piece of a giant puzzle. An example of this is a market for clothes which may consist of male clothes, female clothes, kid's clothes, etc. You can further narrow it down by saying male kid's shorts or female kid's skirts, among others. Defining your niche market signifies that you have a good understanding of what your target market is, along with an understanding of the critical details: what your target market needs, and ways to get their needs to them.

Selecting a niche makes it easier to have targets, promote, and finally, deliver. There will be no point trying to sell female skirts to people who have male kids. A niche will not only make it easier for you to have targets. It will also make good gains. While selecting a niche, the first subject that you think about does not necessarily have to be your niche. If you do this, it might be challenging to make progress. There are ways to select niches, and we will look into this shortly.

Choosing a Niche Market

Your TikTok page should have a reputation for one thing in particular. This might be a topic you are interested in. When selecting a niche, you should choose one that you have a passion for and can go on making posts without any feeling of boredom.

If you find narrowing your niche a little challenging, make a more in-depth search on TikTok. Take time to analyze the best pages that are related to topics you have an interest in. Get to know about the people in these fields, as well as the hashtags they use.

Learning whether a niche is represented on TikTok will make the process of finding a niche a lot easier for you. Now that you know what a niche is and how to find the right one for you, you should get the right audience for your content.

Define Your Audience

Finding out who those you will be talking to are comes just after figuring out what you want to post. There are specific questions you should ask yourself to find your way around this.

- What is the level of engagement I need?

- What type of content can I offer conveniently?

- What is the value I can provide with the interests I have?

- Who is my audience?

- What amount of traffic can I cope with monthly?

With these questions, you can determine your audience. Doing this will help you arrange your content in a way that will be proof that you have the same interests as them. It becomes easy for people to follow you if they can have a relationship with what you post. As a marketer in the cat niche, for example, your content can be focused on cat care, cat scratch pads, etc.

The value you bring to your community is essential. This is because, with it, your followers can decide how relevant you are. This will help them come to a conclusion on how much they need to check your posts. As soon as users discover that they can get the latest information on the things that interest them from you, you will have an increase in traffic.

Come Up with a Strategy

Coming up with a strategy is the next thing to do after developing a niche and an audience. As a starter, you should select a niche and stay there for a while so you can have more followers. This can be done quickly by following users that have similar interests or themes as you.

You should also leave interesting comments when they post. Engaging with an already-existing community will go a long way in helping you have followers. It is only a matter of time before they begin liking your posts and making comments. When you get to this point, what you post becomes essential. Here, you have to make sure every post you put up contains essential and relevant information that is backed up by pictures and videos. If you do this, you will experience an increase in the number of your followers. With a good strategy, having interactions with other pages becomes possible.

Stay Consistent

As soon as you have an increase in followers, staying consistent with what you post is non-negotiable. The time you make a post is important. However, even more important is what you post. Staying for up to a week without any posts will make your followers move to other pages. If you are not sure how frequently you should make posts, check out what other pages in your niche do. After discovering how often they post, the frequency of your own posts should be at least equal to theirs, if not more so.

Ensure Your Niche is Profitable

You have to be aware of the fact that various niches offer various returns. This means the profit level of a niche should also affect your choice of a niche.

A niche can only be profitable if it has the right numbers. The only way to find out this is by asking yourself some questions. These questions are:

- Is it possible to augment a solution that is already on the market?
- Can you make a solution available to a want, problem, or need?
- Are individuals interested in spending their hard-earned money on the niche you are in?
- Are there lots of individuals interested in the niche you have selected?

If you can boldly say "yes" to the questions above, then your niche is profitable. It, however, is still okay if you look into other niches. This is even more important if you want to make a profit over a long time. There are lots of profitable niches. Some of them are discussed below.

Niches that can Make You Money on TikTok

There are quite a number of niches that are popular only for a short while. It is not wrong to follow the trend. However, it is impossible to know when it will stop being trendy. It is much better if you select a niche that is evergreen and will always be profitable.

Below are niches that are profitable and will stand the test of time:

Fitness and Health

People have to stay healthy and fit. This is one reason health and fitness will always be profitable.

You can offer tips and hacks that can help your audience enjoy good health. It is okay if you let your audience in on your own journey to fitness. You can also make suggestions on products that you have used, as well as those others produced.

Travel

A lot of us think of visiting one luxury location after another. There is also a place we are interested in seeing. The travel industry is one you should consider when coming up with a niche. The market for the travel industry is prevalent. Due to this, your niches must be narrowed down if you want to have any impact. Reviewing locations to visit, places to eat, etc., are great ideas for getting started.

Business

Everyone needs money. This is an undeniable fact. If you are very business-inclined, then it wouldn't be a bad idea to try out the business niche. You might be a business coach who offers services that business owners need available or a consultant who offers services to business. At the moment, lots of business owners have accounts on TikTok. This, therefore, makes it a niche you should try out. Just like working on other niches, a high level of focus is required.

Narrow things down as much as you can. Offer how-tos, tricks, and hacks that will add value to the lives of business people. After doing this for a while, you can be sure to have an increased number of followers. These followers will not just be mere followers, but people willing to purchase what you intend on selling. Marketing, blogging, and real estate are some of the most famous niches in the business sector.

Beauty

The beauty industry is vibrant and is made up mostly of ladies. Nonetheless, plenty of men are very much interested in beauty products too, and this will not come to an end anytime soon. One easy way to get started within the beauty industry is by sharing tutorials and product reviews. The beauty sector is a sector that involves lots of visuals. This, therefore, makes it an excellent niche for TikTok.

Fashion

The fashion industry is related to the beauty industry. To take advantage of the fashion sector, you have to discover ways your style stands out. Once you have your style established, go on and set up a business page on TikTok which shows off this unique style. This way, you will not have to struggle to come up with content, as you are just being you. You do not have to be an experienced fashion designer to take advantage of this. If you know how to come up with the ideal look daily, you can focus on the fashion sector. Watches, jewelry, and accessories are some of the best niches in the fashion industry.

Animals

The pet industry in the United States alone made up to $86 billion in 2017. There is an estimate that in the near future, the pet industry will be over $202 billion. Included in this are treats, clothing, pet care, etc.

A lot of people are passionate about animals. They even go to the extent of treating these animals like they are a part of their families. You can take advantage of this by having a thriving TikTok account and catering to these individuals.

Relationships

So long as people exist, relationship drama will never cease. This, therefore, makes the relationship niche one of the most profitable. It is common for people to look for ways in which they can have a better understanding of members of the opposite sex. In addition to trying to know the opposite sex better, people are also looking for ways to improve their relationships. The implication of this is this niche is one with a potential to give you plenty of followers.

Some of the niches under relationships that you can take advantage of are: business relationships, parenting, friends, and romantic relationships. If you have a good number of tips that can help people in their relationships, you can make a good amount of money off of this by sharing those tips on TikTok.

Gaming

Kids are not the only ones who play games. Adults love gaming too. If you know anyone that is in love with games, you can get an estimated value of games in your head.

People who love games go to great lengths to be able to afford these games. They purchase walkthroughs, consoles, guides, and of course, the games themselves. A lot of them go as far as playing games on YouTube, as well as other platforms that make this possible.

A lot of people on TikTok make lots of money reviewing video games. A lot of them do this as a primary job and not just a means to earn money on the side. One of these people is PewDiePie. This TikTok account has over 14 million followers on TikTok. Newcomers can make a lot from this niche too, as it is a vast one.

Luxury and Lifestyle

The fact is, everyone loves to enjoy the beautiful things in life. Do you enjoy snapping pictures of cars, foods, and uploading pictures of your everyday life? This might be the perfect niche for you. This niche is one that involves giving people a peek into the life that many people want to live.

The luxury niche involves displaying glimpses of the high life that virtually everyone is interested in living. You can decide to stick to the lifestyle niche or the luxury niche. These two niches are very organized as well as very profitable. You can narrow your posts to travel, houses, fast cars, sport bikes, etc.

Parenting/Family

This can be considered a spin-off from the relationship industry. It is a niche that is snowballing. You do not have to be a parent to know that parenting is not easy. Parents, both new and old, face lots of challenges when it comes to bringing up their children. Due to this, they are always searching for ways to learn more about parenting. A lot of them would appreciate it if they got the right advice on any products that can make parenting less challenging. Accounts which are centered on this sector are very profitable. The underlying reason for this is that you yourself are from a family. So, you do not need to be a parent to understand the importance of this sector.

Chapter 4: Collaborate with Others

There are numerous influencers on TikTok, and they have a significant number of followers. Armed with the right plan, you can become a famous brand on TikTok. To do this, you must understand how to market your brand on TikTok.

A Business Profile

If you don't, then it is time that you switch to a business profile. Merely go to the settings in your account and enable the "Switch to Business Profile option." Are you wondering why you must switch to a business profile? Here are a couple of benefits you stand to gain. Once you create a business profile, you no longer have to use the advertising tools provided by Facebook for publishing and creating ads on TikTok. A TikTok user can get in touch with you from your TikTok page by clicking on the contact button placed in your profile. It is quite similar to the way anyone can contact you from your official website. Apart from this, it also gives you access to TikTok's analytical tool known as Insights. You can use Insights to track essential metrics like impressions and reach of your account. Once you have a business profile, we can examine all the other steps for successfully marketing your brand on TikTok.

Using TikTok Tools

The business profile is a TikTok are quite similar to those on Facebook. Using insights enables you to view various statistics related to your account and followers like engagement data, impressions, and so on. If you want, it also provides you a detailed breakdown of your follower's demographics. You can get a detailed analysis of demographics like age, gender, active hours, and location of your followers on TikTok. Insights don't have to be generalized, and you can make them as specific as you want them to be. In fact, if you wish, you can get accurate insights about any of your posts on TikTok. This tool comes in handy, especially when you're trying to understand the kind of content that your audience appreciates. The more information you have about your audience's preferences, it becomes easier to connect and interact with them.

Product Teasers

Do you ever watch teasers of any upcoming movies? Do you ever wonder why teasers are made? Well, it is to generate buzz and create curiosity about the movies. Likewise, you can also create product teasers to generate curiosity about products. One of the best places where you can start advertising about any products you offer for sale or services you provide is TikTok. If you understand the nuances of marketing, then you don't have to worry about wooing your potential customers by showing them advertisements about any upcoming products. You must be careful not to be too pushy. If you're too pushy, you will quickly lose your followers. A product is a simple post, which can generate a buzz about the products without making it seem like a hard sell. There is a TikTok account known as the Gilt Man, which is essentially a shopping destination for men. While advertising, they didn't mention anything that might make it seem like they were trying hard to sell. Instead, they came up with a promotional offer wherein customers could download the app and avail amazing discounts. Their TikTok posts consisted of product photos, and their captions mentioned the promotional offer. Each of their posts received tens of thousands of likes. Their TikTok advertisements worked because it didn't come across as being too pushy. Likewise, whenever Starbucks comes up with a seasonal drink, they post pictures on TikTok and provide product teasers without trying to force their followers to make any purchases.

By using product teasers, you don't have to force your audience to take any action. Instead, you are gently coaxing them to take an action you want without making it seem like a hard sell. Since you know that your audience is interested in what you are offering, you are merely trying to tip the scales in your favor. If you keep forcing your audience to do something you want and come on a little too strong, you will merely lose your followers. Posting product photos is a great way to create interest.

Partnering with Influencers

The fastest way to reach potential customers is by partnering with influencers in your niche. Influencers already have an established base of followers. Influencers have become rather popular on TikTok these days. A lot of people are buying products or availing services based on the reviews given by influencers. This happens because an influencer often has the trust of his or her followers. If you manage to partner with the right influencer in your niche, you can certainly generate more publicity about your brand. So, the first step is to identify the most popular influencers in your niche industry. Don't merely concentrate on short-term gains whenever you're working with an influencer. Instead, start thinking about all the long-term benefits this relationship can offer. You not only gain access to an influencer's existing base of followers, but you also get a chance to network and establish a strong relationship with someone who can help you attain your brand's goals.

Never Over-Post

While using TikTok, keep in mind that you must not over post. You might be tempted to start posting several pictures at once. Don't do this. If you start clogging up your follower's feeds with multiple posts on a single day, you will lose their interest. If you do want to post multiple pictures in one go, use the album feature wherein you can create a carousel gram, which includes multiple pictures that are displayed in the format of a slideshow. In this manner, you will not clog up their post or lose their interest. Not only is it important to be mindful of posting content at the right time frames, you also need to ensure you don't post an excessive amount. After all, you are trying to build a brand and not come across as spam page. If you start overwhelming your audience with an excess of content regardless of how wonderful the content is, you will not be able to get more followers. For instance, if you have a TikTok account where you post motivational quotes or life philosophy, it is a good idea to stick to just one post per day. No one is really in the mood to read more than one or two inspirational posts at once. So, keep this in mind whenever you're creating your content schedule.

Sponsored Ads Can Work

TikTok ads have become quite popular these days and rightly so. One of the great things about these ads is that you have complete control over the amount you want to spend on these arts. Essentially, you can budget your ads and stick to the budget. Apart from this, it also gives you the option of selecting the format of the ad. It can be one ad in the form of a sponsored ad or multiple ads in the form of carousel advertising. It not only gives brands a chance to target their customers, but it also curates such advertisements, which will prompt customers to take a specific action you desire. Before the concept of sponsored posts was introduced on TikTok, only those users who were following your account will be unable to see your photos or update. Now, with all the latest updates, brands are free to promote their content to anyone who fits their profile of an ideal customer.

Whenever you want to use sponsored ads, make sure that the content you are using is not only engaging but also appeals to your ideal customer demographic. In fact, even an existing post can be reformatted into a sponsored post. Whenever you notice that certain posts of yours are doing exceptionally well, you can later transform them into a sponsored post.

User-Submitted Content

Wouldn't it be rather wonderful if you could create content without having to do the necessary groundwork? Well, you can do this. The simplest way to gain content is by curating user-generated photos. If you already have an audience who is engaged with your brand, this becomes quite easy. You can always leverage your audience to create content for your brand. User-generated content is not as helpful to the brands, but it is quite engaging for users as well. Did you know that the cosmetics giant MAC uses user-generated content regularly? Whenever you use user-generated content, you are essentially providing validation to your followers. If you're wondering how you can get your followers to create content without coming across as being too pushy, then don't worry. It is pretty simple. Your followers are also interested in increasing the following on TikTok, just like you. So, by letting them know that you will be tagging them in your posts whenever you regram, it is a great incentive for your audience. GoPro does this quite frequently and even has a branded hashtag for it-#featuredphotographereveryweek.

Tracking the Right Metrics

If you want to improve the performance of your TikTok posts and optimize them, then it is essential to understand how your page, as well as the posts, are performing. Well, how do you do this? You can do this by tracking TikTok metrics like follower growth rate. Concentrating on the total number of followers that you have might seem vain, but the metric of follower growth rate is different from the number of followers you have. By keeping an eye on the growth rate of your following, you can analyze the effect the kind of content you post has on your followers. Another metric that you must always keep track of is the engagement rate. The number of likes or comments that every TikTok post earns influences the engagement rate. You can start curating content or creating content that is similar to the post with the highest engagement rate.

Apart from these two metrics, there's a third metric that you must watch out for, and that is the click-through rate. Before you can start tracking the click-through rate or CTR, you must have a business website. The CTR showcases the number of people who have clicked on the URL you have placed in the TikTok bio of your brand's profile. There's a direct correlation between the effectiveness of your marketing tactics on TikTok and the CTR. The higher the effectiveness of the marketing strategy, the higher the CTR be. You will learn more about TikTok metrics subsequently.

Relate to Your Followers

Yes, it is quite essential to create content that will appeal to your target audience. In fact, spend some time and come up with the ideal description of your target audiences well. If you post content with your target audience alike, it is quite likely that your followers will increase. However, the content that you post must also be in sync with your brand's objective purpose.

For instance, let us assume that you offer financial consulting services. You spend some time and come up with the ideal buyer persona. Your buyer persona helped determine that your target audience loves sports cars and follow profiles that relate to sports cars. So, you might be thinking that you should start posting pictures of sports cars. Well, this might sound like a good idea in theory, but as a practical solution, it isn't that good. After all, your brand claims to be offering financial consulting services, yet your TikTok is full of pictures of sports cars. This doesn't sound like a good marketing strategy, does it? Therefore, it is quintessential to strike a balance between being able to relate to your customers while staying relevant to your brand. So, are you wondering what you can do? Well, since you know that your target audience like sports cars, you must come up with content that stays relevant to your brand while appealing to your target audience. You can create a post that includes a wonderful picture of a sports car along with a description that brings in a financial perspective to the same. Maybe you can add a caption that says they should probably hire your financial consulting services so that they can purchase the sports car that is shown in the picture.

Well, if you start following all the tips that are given in this section, you will certainly be able to increase the number of followers you have on TikTok. Don't be under any misconceptions that you will be able to increase your following overnight. It will take some time, patience, and consistent effort. The results will certainly be worth your while, so make an effort.

Chapter 5: Increase the Commitment of Your Followers

Generally speaking, the word expert and the word authority are used interchangeably, this is not the case with affiliate marketing, however, where being an authority provides you with countless benefits and being an expert counts for little if anything in the long run. Specifically, in this case, an expert is someone who knows a lot about a certain niche, while authority is the person that all of the experts agree is the first stop for information on a given niche. To put it another way, authorities aren't authorities because they say they are, they are authorities because when they make declarations in regard to their niche of choice, other people listen.

While being known as an expert in your chosen niche or sub-niche is impressive, there are plenty of other experts hanging around, but there can only ever be a small number of authorities (by definition). If you can find yourself in this position, then you can expect plenty of eyes on your website and legions of adoring fans. As such, in this position, you will be able to stop worrying about looking for ways to grow your audience and can rest assured that those in your chosen niche will seek you out instead.

A large part of becoming an authority is ensuring that the level of trust between you and your readers is at the point where they can essentially take everything you say as fact. The most surefire way for someone to build their authority is always to be right, not just sometimes, or even most of the time, but every single time you make a definitive statement. When you finally make it to the point where you have earned the trust of those who visit your site, you will want to hold it as the gold standard of importance and never do anything to make these people think less of you.

Be Mindful of Tone:

While you should already know what type of content your target audience will be expecting, how you present this information is going to be equally vital when it comes to showing them that you are just alike, except for the fact that you know more than they do. To accomplish this task, you are going to want to make an extra effort to get into their minds, speak as they speak, think as they think, and use the same references that they use to relate to one another. The easiest way to do so is to consult your demographic data and pick the largest section of it to adopt as your own.

If your target audience is under 30, then the best way to ensure that you are all on the same page is to visit YouTube.com and listen to the current tastemakers on the niche in question. If you have a niche that is focused more on those over 30, then the time you spent studying the niche should be enough to push you in the right direction. Assuming your target audience is younger, then you will want to watch videos made by content creators with the most views as this shows that they are doing something that the target audience really responds to. Understanding the sound of your target audience will make your claim to authority more believable because you will sound like a peer rather than a researcher.

Once you have the language and tone down pat, the next thing you will need to do is to go over the image you are presenting to your target audience with a fine-tooth comb. Additionally, you will want to consider what, aside from being an authority, you are trying to convince your target audience of and what you are trying to get them to do.

Tones to try

•*Informal:* It is best not to start out with an informal tone right out of the gate as new readers can be put off by what can feel like an unearned familiarity. It is fine to adopt it over time; however, you will need to be careful to ensure you maintain your authority at the same time. The best way to do so is to ensure you remain passionate and enthusiastic about your topic while mixing in more detailed insight with the more relaxed phrasing.

•*Promotional:* While you will certainly want to promote new products or services as they come online, it is easy to go back to this well far too often if you are not careful which means it is important to be especially cautious about rolling out this type of content early on as you don't want those who stumble across your site to assume it is full of nothing but longer advertisements for your products. Regardless of the content you are creating, it is important to ensure you always maintain your authority throughout by including specific, niche reasons that make the products or services that you are selling worth your customers' time.

•*Formal:* This is the tone you are likely going to want to start with when you start creating content for your business blog. While it is certainly appropriate during the early days, you are likely going to want to slip into something at least a little more informal over time because you want your customers to feel as though they are talking to a friend when they interact with your content, not as though they are being lectured at. While this is an easy way to make it sound as though you are an authority figure, it is the type of authority figure that people listen to because they are forced too, not because they want to.

•*Consider your voice:* Every content creator has a unique voice, a "one-of-a-kind" perspective on the world that comes through in their word choice and their phrasing. In an extremely competitive online environment, properly honing your tone can be the difference between being an authority and being just another faceless expert. You are what sets your content apart from any other, do everything you can to ensure it is unique and compelling as possible. If you aren't sure what the right voice for you is, consider the following.

The best place to start is by making a list of all the words that you feel other people would use to describe you. You should spend some time on each of these words and consider how you might make each as clear as possible when it comes to showcasing your personality in what you write. From there, you may be able to add in the written equivalent of any unique speech patterns that you have. These can be difficult to pick out for yourself, which means you are likely going to need some outside input for the best results. You can express these types of things, including the sentence structure that you use, the way you separate your paragraphs, the length of your sentences and more. It is perfectly alright if you can't come up with much right now, the longer you keep at it, the more unique your writing will naturally become.

If you can't come up with much of a voice early on, it is important to let it develop naturally rather than forcing it. Having a forced voice will only limit your voice from developing naturally and essentially paint you into a corner as if you change it once people have gotten used to it you will risk losing their trust.

Share What You Are Reading:

Another great way to build up the idea that you are an authority in your field is to share what you have been reading. You are taking all of this time learning about the ins and outs of your portion of your niche, and you may as well brag a little as it will only make readers think more of you. Dropping a list of names they have never heard of will help cement the idea that you really know what you are talking about.

Before you share the sources of the information you are iterating upon, it is important to vet them thoroughly to ensure everything is as valid as it first appears. Especially early on, you don't want to accidentally stumble upon a so-called expert that is really a fraud that the community as a whole dismissed years ago. Specifically, this means understanding just who created any and all content you plan on referencing, along with their general level of authority within the niche as a whole.

If you pick a reliable source, then you can guarantee that it will be easy to verify, while also helping you to ensure you aren't accidentally opening a well-known can of worms within the niche community. While this will certainly take some work, if doing so ends up saving your burgeoning career as an authority within your niche, then it will be well worth it.

Spread the Word:

After you have dutifully created content for several months, you will finally have all the pieces in place to show your niche audience the extent of your authority. To get started, you are going to want to become a regular presence on the most popular forums where people gather to discuss the niche. This means you are going to want to join the forums and regularly join the conversation, answer questions, and create posts that other people approve of. Making sure to credit your site with the information each time you do.

During this stage it is important to not pander for any of your products and services at this time, becoming an authority isn't about direct marketing like that, the additional sales are something that happens organically and trying to force it will only delay or stagnate the process. After you start seeing forward momentum and increased traffic from all your hard work, you are going to want to implement the final stage of the plan, which means you are going to want to make sure everything about your site and its content is in tip-top shape before you do.

Once you are ready to really put your best foot forward, the final thing you will want to do is to seek out the websites of other experts in the niche and strike up a conversation. Once you have made nice with the neighbors, the next thing you will do is offer to do them a favor; specifically, you will offer to write them a guest blog. As you will no doubt know by this point, keeping a blog can be a significant strain if you don't stick to a strict plan, which means the other experts will likely gladly take you up on your offer.

This will not only make their lives easier in terms of content creation, but it will also establish you as an authority in the niche to that expert's audience because of your broad reach. Once you have reached out to a new audience, it is important to continue interacting with them in a way that will make them want to subscribe to your own newsletter as opposed to getting their information secondhand. This means creating an active TikTok presence and maintaining it in the long term. Just like a blog, having an active TikTok presence that reflects your authoritative status is important to looking professional and having a stale TikTok page indicates that you are no longer on the top of your game.

While you can repost content as part of your TikTok presence, you need to really take advantage of the social aspect of the platform and make as many direct connections as you can make. It is one thing to be the type of authority that puts out decrees from an ivory tower; it is much more effective to be an authority that is seen as being out and amongst the people.

Chapter 6: How to Drive Your Tiktok Followers to Instagram And Youtube

Perhaps the essential part of being on TikTok is growing your following so that you can have an audience to market to. You have contributed to your ability to grow your following and increase your outreach. There are still several things that you can do to improve your TikTok account. Start seeing higher engagement rates. In this case, you are going to discover what it takes to grow your following and start generating success through your TikTok account.

Encouraging Engagement on Your Page

The first thing that you can do to start increasing your audience is to encourage people to engage with you on your page. Remember, the TikTok algorithm favors it when people engage on other users' pages, which means that if you can get your followers to start engaging with you, then that would be good. You can feel confident that they are going to start seeing more of your content, too. You can encourage engagement in two different ways:

engaging with others and asking for engagement from your followers.

When you engage with the people who follow you regularly, they feel more inclined to engage with your posts because they begin to feel the development of a relationship. The back-and-forth support between you and your audience becomes a regular part of your relationship. When you go out of your way to go through your follower list and start engaging with people, you actually "break the ice" between yourself and them. This makes them feel more comfortable and engaged with you and your brand. You can do this by regularly going through your list of followers and tapping on random accounts and engaging with their content. Leaving a few heartfelt comments and liking some of their recent posts is an excellent opportunity to start engaging with people. This also inspires them to like back your content the next time they see your content. As you post, you can also ask for engagement by saying things like, "We love summer! Do you?" This encourages people to speak up. You can also increase engagement by writing captions that say things, like, "Comment with your favorite _____!" or "Tag a friend who would love this, too!"

Asking your followers to engage with your content in this way helps them break their thought process from mindless scrolling. Instead, you help them choose to participate in your content. Another great way to encourage engagement is to run giveaways on your page. This allows you to set rules that require individuals to engage with your post to enter the giveaway. Often, companies will decide on what they want to give away. Then they will set the requirements for individuals. For example, "Follow us, tag a friend, and share this post to your stories to enter in the giveaway!" Then, they will leave the giveaway for a certain period, allowing them to experience plenty of engagement from their followers. This type of behavior drives up engagement on that one post, but it will also support you in driving up engagement on the rest of your posts as well. You do not want to be engaging in too many giveaways, however. Two to four giveaways per year are plenty, and this is a great way to get involved with more followers.

Regularly Updating Your Following List

The people and the hashtags whom you follow are the ones that populate your main home screen, which allows you to see images that everyone you are following shares posts regularly. You want to ensure that you are regularly updating your following list so that you are only seeing people who reflect those that are actually associated with your branding or positioning. You might feel inspired to follow personal interests on TikTok, but this is typically best reserved for private personal accounts instead of business accounts. You want to ensure that your time spent scrolling through your followed accounts is spent investing in the growth of your business so that this becomes productive in the long run.

You can update your following list by going through the people you follow and unfollowing anyone who does not make sense to your brand. This way, you are not seeing content that is entirely irrelevant to you or following accounts that are unlikely to provide you with any return on your engagement. You can only support or unfollow up to 60 accounts in an hour, so take your time with this, and do it regularly so that you do not have many changes to make to your account. It would help if you were doing this every week so that you are staying relevant in your industry and seeing the latest trends and people who are coming up. Once you have unfollowed everyone who is not connected to you, you can start going to your most popular hashtags. See if there are any new hashtags or followers for you to pay attention to through the top posts in these searches. This way, you can start following new users who may support you in bringing more attention to your account each time you engage with their content or interact with them.

In addition, when you follow new hashtags that are trending in your niche, you can keep tabs on what's hot. You can also go ahead and start using those hashtags on your photographs so that you can stay relevant, as well. This type of research creates two powerful opportunities for growth in one move, so it is worthy of your regular attention and time!

Saying the Right Thing at the Right Time

On TikTok, you need to make sure that you are answering the right thing at the right time. By posting the right content at the right time, you can ensure that you stay relevant and that your content relates to what your audience is going through or thinking about. Your audience will be likely paying attention to and engaging with your content. The easiest way to say the right thing at the right time on TikTok is by following your audience.

Paying Attention to the Trends

Pay attention to the latest trends, concerns, and issues. That may be arising that people are paying attention to. For example, if you are in the blogging industry and you blog about current events concerning famous people, you would want to stay up-to-date on all of the latest trends and gossip. You would also want to blog about them as soon as they reach your eyes. The same would go for any industry that you are in. The moment you see a trend or topic waving through your industry, you need to be prepared to get on board with it, customize how you share it according to your unique brand, and offer it as soon as possible. In addition to following unexpected trends that arise in your industry, you also need to be following expected trends like holidays or scheduled events that are relevant to your audience. For example, if you are in the fashion industry, you should be paying attention to popular fashion events like Fashion Week and the Victoria Secret Fashion Show. If you are in the tech industry, you should be paying attention to the latest device launches and information regarding events that are big in the tech industry, like the annual E3 event.

These types of events occur consistently, and they are extremely helpful in allowing you to stay relevant in your industry. Pay attention to the information being released by those who drive the industry like influencers and developers. It is important that you avoid talking about things out of season or out of turn, as sharing information too long after the event occurred can result in coming across as irrelevant or outdated. Typically, people who see companies sharing outdated information will believe that this company is not paying attention and does not care enough to stay in the loop with what is going on in their industry. As a result, people will not follow you. Remember, we live in the digital age where information can become available fast, and trends can rise and fall even more quickly. It would help if you were ready to get into these trends and start creating your brand's name in the heat of the moment, not after the trend or information has already started declining in popularity.

If you find that staying with the trends is harder than it looks, try finding three to four people or blogs. Follow those who are always quick to jump into new trends and pay attention to these individuals or resources. This way, you are not overwhelming yourself by trying to follow too many people at once, becoming lost in what is relevant, what is a trend, and what is entirely irrelevant to you and your audience.

Targeting Your Audience Through Your Words

You now know that TikTok's biggest way to target audiences is through hashtags. This is how you can reach new audience members and start growing your audience fast. However, there is another verbal element that comes into play when it comes to creating an impact through your captions and writing. This is by having words in your captions that resonate with your audience.

You do not want to be using words that do not make sense to your audience or that sound completely irrelevant or outdated. This will lead to your audience becoming disinterested in reading what you have to say and struggling to actually "follow" what you are trying to tell them.

The best way to speak like your audience is to pay attention to what they care about by following them back and listening to how they are speaking. Regularly scroll through your feed and read what the people you follow are saying so you can get a feel for what their language is like, how they tone their messages, and if there are any unique slang words, phrases, or acronyms that they are using to connect with their audiences. The more you read your niche's captions and comments, the more you are going to become familiar with how they are speaking, what they are saying, and what they are reading. This way, you can begin emulating their language through your posts and saying things in a way that makes sense to your audience.

When you do start emulating your audience, there are a few things that you will need to refrain from doing to avoid having your audience tune out from what you are saying. One thing to remember is that you need to prevent emulating your audience to the point that you lose your authenticity because you sound like you are identical to those whom they are already reading. Make sure that you pay attention to your brand's voice and your mission statement and adapt the industry's language to meet your tone and not the other way around. If your mood seems too off-base for your industry, you can consider casually adjusting it slightly to fit the industry's needs more. But do not begin changing your approach too frequently, or you will come across as fake and untrustworthy. The second thing that you need to avoid doing is creating messages that are filled with industry jargon that your general following is unlikely to understand.

If you attempt to use industry jargon that is commonly used between those who sell products and services in the industry, but that is unlikely to be recognizable by those who purchase in or follow the industry, you may lose your following solely because they do not understand you. You do not want to be creating gaps and confusion in your marketing by using language that your audience does not know because this can make it unnecessarily challenging for people to follow you and support your business. Keep it simple, speak in a way that your audience will understand, and adapt the industry language to suit your brand's message and purpose.

Leveraging TikTok Stories

TikTok Stories are a powerful tool that can be used not only to nurture your existing following but also to attract new followers for your business. When you use your TikTok stories correctly, you can create a significant influx of engagement from your followers and add a personal opportunity to connect with your brand. It also allows you to create a more interactive page overall. On TikTok, people love interacting with the brands that they love and consuming as much of their content as they can, and TikTok offers plenty of ways for followers to do just that. As you upload stories throughout the day, you create the opportunity for your followers to feel like you are genuinely thinking about them throughout the day, which establishes a connection of care and compassion between you and your followers. Not only will this help you maintain your existing followers, but it will also help new or potential followers see how interactive and intimate you are with your following, which leads to them wanting to be a part of your audience as well!

The reason that stories work is simple. People are nosy, and they like to know the insider's information. This is not a bad thing either, but rather just a simple human experience where we all desire to be a part of something bigger than ourselves. And we want to connect with those around us to become a part of that "something bigger." You can position yourself as the facilitator of that "something bigger" by turning your brand into an experience that people can enjoy and an entity that they can share an intimate and compassionate relationship with. Stories give you a great option to do that because every picture or short clip you share reflects a part of your personal behind-the-scenes experiences. You can also curate your story feed to offer an even more exclusive and intimate feel by purposefully sharing things that will allow others to feel like they are genuinely connected with you through your feed.

The key to making your stories intimate and leveraging them to attract new followers and maintain your existing ones is to make sure that the content you share in your stories is exclusive and unlike anything that you are sharing anywhere else. Be very intentional in sharing things that are more personal and "private" than what you would share on IGTV or on your feed itself because this way, people feel like they truly are getting that private insight into your brand. TikTok stories are already somewhat exclusive because, after 24 hours, they are gone and cannot be viewed again. You can play up that exclusivity thing by sharing the right content, mentioning things that you shared previously that new followers can no longer see, and even by suggesting outright that your story feed is exclusive. Say things like, "Keep your eyes on my stories because I will be announcing an exclusive offer here first... Get it three days earlier just by watching the story!" or something similar to this. Another way that you can leverage TikTok Stories is by making story highlights which can enable your new followers to see exclusive tidbits of your previous stories.

So, if you are someone who regularly travels, and you often share intimate travel experiences with people, such as the restaurants you dine at or the people you meet, you might consider sharing these in your stories. Then, you can create highlights of certain moments from your travels that were most exciting or interesting so that your new audience can glance back through your stories and start feeling more intimately connected with you right away. Leveraging your highlight reels in this way is a great opportunity to show your new followers what to expect, give them that feeling of having known you and your brand for a long time already, and increase their interest in you right from the start.

Using IGTV to Increase Your Following

IGTV is a great way to increase your following. These videos stay in place for as long as you leave them up, which means that followers can look back through your IGTV channel and watch stuff that you put up days, weeks, months, or even years ago once it has been around long enough. You can leverage IGTV to create new followers by creating excellent IGTV videos and then promoting them elsewhere on the net so that people are more likely to click over to your channel and watch. Once they see your video and the quality of the content you create, they can choose to follow your page to get more if they decide that they like you. The big opportunity with IGTV is that you can promote your IGTV channel just like you would a YouTube channel or any other free video content on the net.

By creating great content and then sharing it around the net, you can encourage individuals to go over to your TikTok to be able to actually see the video. This means that you can funnel people from Facebook, Twitter, Snapchat, email, and any other social media platform to TikTok so that they can catch your free content and learn from it. To make your content accessible, you need to make sure that the IGTV videos you make are worthy of receiving views. In other words, you need to create high-quality and engaging content. Your audience wants to pay attention so that when you share it with other platforms. They are more likely to click through your channel and watch the content that you created.

Chapter 7: Build Your Brand or Collaborate with Other Brands

During the early days, you are likely going always to feel strapped for resources. As such, it is important to focus first on creating a brand, as it will ultimately influence almost every other facet of your operation. These days a good brand is the sum total of the way your social media presence looks and feels and also determines who it speaks too and thus who your follower base is going to be. Regardless of the type of social media account you are planning on starting, your brand identity should be given a serious thought. While the specifics of what constitutes brand identity can be a bit vague, you can assume it includes graphics and visual presentation, design, iconography, typography, color palette, and logo. There are certainly other elements you can include in this list, but these should be enough to get you moving in the right direction.

Think hard about your target audience: When it comes to building a brand, the first thing you are going to want to do is to determine who your target audience is going to be. This is largely going to be influenced by the niche you've chosen, as well as the items that you have your eye on selling. When determining who your target audience is going to be, you are going to want to start by talking to social media and seeing what sorts of people are talking about the products you are thinking about selling.

It is important to really do your research during this step as you want to identify as many interconnected characteristics that you can target amongst those most likely to buy your products for the best results. If you are already a part of this group, then even better, if not, once you have a clear idea of who you are targeting, you are going to want to find out everything about them. This means the types of products they enjoy and what their buying habits are, but also what type of design tends to appeal to their demographic and what their thoughts, and values are more likely to be.

If your target audience is under the age of 40, a good way to do this is to go to YouTube and see what type of content is being produced that is related to your target niche. This will give you a good idea of what type of tone is likely to appeal to your target audience and also what type of phrasing and slang to use in your branding.

Choosing a name

While it doesn't take much to pick out a bad username when you see it, understanding what it takes to create a good name can be much more complicated. To get started, you may want to consider which of the three primary name conventions, whimsical, evocative or descriptive, that you want to explore more fully. Descriptive names are self-explanatory, much like the names themselves and include what the primary focus of the account will be. Alternately you can go with something evocative without really being descriptive, which will prevent you from having to stick to a narrowly defined topic.

Know what's popular: When it comes to creating a useful username, it will automatically make it easier for you to attract new followers if people can find you by simply searching for your primary niche. The best way to go about picking out the optimal search terms for your niche is to utilize a website like UberSuggest.org. All you need to do is enter any word into its search bar and it will provide you with all of the most popular search terms related to it.

Consider related words: If you don't have anything catchy in mind right off the bat, the first thing you are going to consider is words that are naturally related to your niche while also reflecting your unique take on it. A thesaurus of either the physical or digital sort is a great place to start and you never know when a new word might spark the creative notion that gives birth to your new business name. If nothing jumps out at you right from the start, simply make a list of between 50 and 100 potential options and save them for later.

Cast a wide net: Once you have a decent list of words at your disposal, you are going to want to start playing around with them in such a way that they start generating some ideas. A good place to start is with names based around puns. Regardless of how you feel about puns personally, they are a great starting off point and will serve to get your brain in the right type of name creating mindset. Pungenerator.org is a great place to start, just be aware that you may need to put in some time before anything worthwhile surfaces.

Don't end up in a hurry to choose something: If you end up spending an undue amount of time trying to come up with the right name, it can be easy to lose focus and wander off onto a path of logic that no user is going to be able to follow you down. This is why it is important to test the name with other people for a few days to ensure that they pick up what you are laying down. Talk about the name with your friends and family, text it, email it, write it down, try it with different fonts and different sizes to see what you think about it from as many angles as possible. If things work out, then great; otherwise, you will need to be ready to go back to the drawing board and start from scratch.

Create a logo

When it comes to creating a successful logo, the first thing you will need to keep in mind is just how omnipresent that it is going to be. In addition to being on all of your products, it is going to be on all of your email correspondence as well as on any advertising that you might want to pay for down the line. This means that the most important consideration of all is always going to be picking something that is malleable enough to expand or contract as needed. After that, consider the colors and fonts that will speak to your target audience most directly.

A perfect logo is one that can be immediately linked to a specific brand, and the company that sells it. When it is created with the right amount of care, a good logo can represent the values and mission statement of your business as well, all with just a single look. If a picture is worth a thousand words, a good logo is worth a thousand conversions, but only if it is done properly. In many cases, a great place to start is a common symbol that potential customers are likely to encounter in their daily interactions as well as on your labels.

If your marketing is successful, then your target audience will think of your brand whenever that symbol presents itself, essentially hijacking any other purpose that symbol might have. If you don't think that is likely, consider #. Did you think of that as the phrase "pound key" or did you simply see a hashtag? Twitter took # and if you claim a symbol of your own, your target audience won't be able to get away from your brand even if you try.

Additionally, you are going to want a logo that is bold as well as vibrant in such a way that it is sure to catch the eye of any potential customers when they see it as part of your marketing campaign. It also needs to be both clear and visually simple enough for potential customers to instantly have an idea of what they are looking at, so they can absorb your branding instead of scratching their heads over just what it is they are looking at.

Consider your message: The first thing you will want to take some time to think about is the message that you want your logo to convey clearly. This is going to be something fairly straightforward as anything complicated is likely to get lost in the shuffle. If you are having trouble, consider the reason that you wanted to start your website in the first place and then think about the ways that you can sum up your goal in a single sentence. Keep this single sentence handy and refer to it from time to time to ensure everything is staying on message.

Beyond determining what you want to communicate about your brand, you will also need to consider the tone you will want to present as well. This decision shouldn't be made in a vacuum, it should be based on your goals for your site as well as what other people in your niche are currently up to as well.

Develop a mission statement

When combined with a value proposition, a quality mission statement will ensure you leave a good first impression on visitors to your site about your contributions to the world at large. The following guidelines will help you craft a quality mission statement.

Aim big: Good mission statements should be about something bigger than yourself that should ideally connect you and your potential customers emotionally. The thing you choose should matter in the big picture, it also helps if it is something your company actually does.

Be the best: The mission statement you create should be one that makes it clear you are striving to do more than simply be the best at what you do. This type of statement is inward-focused when instead, it needs to be outward-facing and put the customer first.

Focus on what's tangible: The best mission statements don't make grand claims, they focus on the connection that customers have to the business based on their products or services, creating a tangible link that the customer can hold onto as a promise of future growth.

Be yourself: Your mission statement should be as unique as your company. It should express what you do in a clear way that goes beyond just listing the facts. Your mission statement should reflect your brand and everything that makes what you offer so wonderful and unique.

Putting it all together: While creating value is crucial to grow your business in the long-term, making it clear what it is you do exactly is crucial when it comes to getting customers to choose you over your competition. Once you have successfully created your value statement, it is important to look at it from every angle and ensure it is as focused on the customer as possible. If you find that what you created talks more about the company than the clients, then you are going to want to go back to the drawing board and try again. To ensure you get it right, make it a point of reading it as if you were someone who had never visited your site before today.

Additional social media considerations

Branding successfully on social media is an achievable goal. To get the most out of the social media platforms, a company needs to:

- *Develop a strong voice:* Your brand's personality and voice should reflect in every message and post that is being put on the business social media page. Be authentic, be genuine and be true to your brand. Do not fall into the trap of trying to copying another brand's voice and style of presenting itself on social media. What works for one brand may not work for your brand. Find your own voice, find your own style, and be consistent in the way that voice is delivered to your audience so they will come to associate it with your brand.
- *Connect with the audience:* Speak to them as if they matter. Because they do. They are the heart and soul of any business and without an audience, there would be no business. Speak to them and connect with them on their terms, and develop brand messages and posts that they can relate with to strengthen your brand.
- *Post useful content:* Posting multiple times a day with frivolous information that does

nothing to strengthen your brand image is just going to be a waste of time. Content needs to be original, useful and engaging.

- *Engage, engage, engage:* Always engage with your audience and your customers. If they comment on a social media posting, respond. If the comments are positive, thank them and let them know they're appreciated. And if the comments are negative, apologize, be sincere and let them know what steps the business is taking to make the necessary changes. Allow your social media follows to post feedback on your platforms so other users will be able to see. Be transparent and audiences will resonate more with the business.

Find the keywords to SEO your website

Once the basics of your site have been established, all that is left to do is lay the foundation for successful Search Engine Optimization (SEO) in the future. The better the SEO of your site, the better your search engine ranking which means the more new potential customers you can bring in without actively seeking them out. To get started, you will want to go to the Setting menu, found from the Dashboard, and choose the option titled Home.

Here you will need to include a title, a detailed description using keywords of your chose as well as the Meta keywords that will ultimately be displayed. The title should be short and sweet while still including your primary keyword and should always be fewer than 60 total characters. Your Meta description is what will be seen when your site is shown via a search engine, and you need to be concise as you only have 160 characters to work with here. Finally, you will want to include specific keywords separated by commas. If you aren't quite sure which keywords to use, consider the following tips to ensure you are headed in the right direction:

Start by checking with Google: As the primary way that new potential customers will be stumbling upon your content, it makes sense that Google is also the first place to look for relevant keywords. All you need to do is enter the name of your general niche into the search bar and see what options fill in automatically. It is important to take note of what comes up both while you are typing the phrase and after you have included it in its entirety. These can be considered the major topics that people turn to when it comes to your niche so it will typically behoove you to include them in your site.

Once you are done at the top of the page, scroll down to the bottom of the first page of results for a list of other searches that are related to the search you have just finished conducting. While all of these may not be related to your take on the niche in question, they should still give you a few useful takeaways as well as ideas for how to expand your site in the future logically. Your goal from this exercise should be to come up with approximately 5 strong keywords to base your SEO strategy around, having too many keywords will only hurt you in the long run. So, it is important to narrow your choices down right away.

Consider what Wikipedia thinks: Additionally, you will want to visit Wikipedia to determine what it thinks are the most relevant keywords to your niche. Wikipedia has become one of the top-ranked websites across the entire world without putting a single cent into advertising and this is solely because they really know what they are doing when it comes to maximizing their SEO. Start by typing your nice into the search bar, if it brings up a direct result great, otherwise add the name of whatever page it links to your list of words.

From there, you will want to consider the first paragraph overview of the content in question. This paragraph generally provides a brief glimpse at the content of the article in general complete with every possible link to additional content that could be relevant to the search in question. Depending on your take on the niche, every single one of those words could be used in your keyword search, and the hard part is narrowing them down.

The search function on your site: While this won't necessarily be useful right off the bat, once your site has been around long enough to start drawing in some traffic, pouring over your own search data will show you the types of things that people who visit your site are looking for with no ifs and or buts. You can find these results from your Google Analytics page and using this information to improve your SEO is highly recommended once you have the opportunity to do so.

More Google: Google Correlate, available at Google.com/Trends/Correlate can help you to more easily determine what related topics the people interested in your niche are also interested in. For example, if your niche is related to outdoor exploration, then you might find that people who are interested in outdoor exploration are also interested in survival prepping. Not only will the program show you just which keywords are searched in related searches but also just how often each of those searches was performed. The program even breaks down the usage of specific keywords to various geographic locations, allowing you to pinpoint the particular interests of your audience even more readily.

Chapter 8: How to Create Content That Sells Your Or Other People's Product

Using templates can help you create great content and it helps so much when you are trying to produce better content. There are a lot of websites that offer some great templates and you will be able to change them to suit your needs as they come. If you use these, you do not even have to exert much effort and it can look incredible.

If you desire to establish a post that is, going to endorse a special offer, this is also a great idea because maybe you need a template to announce a new opening time or maybe you want to push a recipe that you have been able to share on a blog. Whatever message you need to send, you can do it with the template and there are some great places that you can find them for free. You can edit copy and select them and you can do different colors and styles as well. It is a great way to make some real quality content on your TikTok. You can also find high-quality stock images as well for help. Stock images have a bit of a bad rap in new times, but that has not to say that you should avoid utilizing them. They can actually aid make a diverse feed that will use other images and other templates. However, not all stock images have what it takes to be a prime spot in your feed. Some are honestly pretty terrible and you need to make sure that their royalty-free.

You need high-quality photos that actually do not look stocky. There are a couple of different places that you can go and they offer a wide range of images for free. Because of this, you are bound to find something suitable, whatever you are niche. Once again, just make sure that the images are royalty-free; otherwise, you could be suffering from copyright infringement. Now on this same idea, if you want to make unique stock images, you can also customize them by using overlays, filters, and icons on borders. Whatever it is that you like to do is what works and will be good for you.

You can repost TikTok content from brands within your niche as well. If you do not have time to generate your personal content, the good news is you may not have to. It might be the incident that other TikTok accounts are already doing a great job of producing amazing content that your audience is actually interested in, and if you get permission from the brands to do so, you can repost them. When you can repost the content that is similar to yours or from an account that is relevant to your audience, just make sure that you get their permission first. You always have to reach out to the user for permission to repost because it is their content that you want to repost. As such, you cannot simply steal it, and you need to make sure that you are approaching this through the proper way and making sure that you obtain their permission before you do anything with their content.

Once you reposted if you have permission to do so, you will need to give them the proper credit. Tag them and make sure that you are following the proper channels to do this correctly. Sharing videos and stories to your feed is another great way of creating content as well. Everyone loves to see the stories and everyone loves to see the videos because that makes them feel like they are closer to you and that they have a real connection with you. It is also a great thing to do because people love seeing the video and our brains usually want to see this first in many cases. Pictures are great, but you can be really drawn into a video in a way that a picture might not be able to do for you. However, on the flip side to this, you can be really drawn into a photo, whereas you might not be drawn into a video.

Another great idea for good content is to use user-generated content. We talked about this a little bit before, but the term applies to any content created by a user or any product or service that is about that product or service that the user is trying to create. Unless you are a giant or prominent brand, its likely users will create TikTok content about you and your products without an incentive. Get around this by running a competition where users could actually win something by creating a TikTok post about you.

Offering a follower a free product or a discount, for instance, will really gain traction. If you are running a campaign where users can win something, you will notice that they are creating posts and following your hashtags so that they can see what is going on with the contest. You can also publish your competition across your other social media channels or even include in a newsletter if you wanted to and you can monitor the performance of your campaign hashtag to see how well the contest is going as well, and you can do this simply by using tools that TikTok offers free. You should not be too exclusive with the kind of content you request your users to post. Otherwise, the users are not going to bother. User-generated content should have an augmented method to source and content for your feed instead of being the focus. This is important because if you rely too much on user-generated content, your followers may feel like you are exploiting them and you will have less control over the aesthetic of your feed.

Collaborations with influencers is another great way to get your content to be the best that it can be. If you want more control over your feed and you need a consistent flow of on-brand TikTok content, you should seriously consider trying to work with influencers. If you collaborate with influencers that already have good-sized following, let them come to you. You have a great opportunity here to expand your following.

You would also have some great feed content that you can use to your advantage. If you are a small business with a small business budget or a small brand with a small brand budget, then obviously, you will want to connect with a micro-influencer rather than a big-name influencer. Micro-influencers usually have a following of people between ten thousand or even up to fifty thousand, and it is very easy to strike a deal with them. However, the important thing to remember is that this is true only if you are what is known as a TikTok seller.

This means only if you are selling a product on TikTok or if your brand is selling something on TikTok that their audience is going to be genuinely interested in. If they know that their audience is not going to be interested in what your niche is, then they are not going to go with you. This is why you need to find an influencer that fits your niche and fits it well. So, for example, if your niche is fitness, you may not be able to work with someone whose niche is traveling. This is because fitness and traveling do not necessarily go together. They can be brought together, but it is not something that you typically see.

If you are a small brand, you are working with fitness, and you see a micro-influencer that has a following because they are posting workout routines, you are more likely to be able to work with them because you are both into fitness and your niches are similar. You can send a DM, which is like a private message on TikTok, and usually, influencers will have their contact information in their bio as well if you need them. Send them a private message and see if they would be willing to work with you and more often than not, they're very kind and they're actually more likely to work with you so that they're able to experience some benefits as well and not just give you benefit.

One of the biggest reasons that you should be using TikTok for business and branding is to check out the facts. If you consider TikTok compared to other social media platforms like Twitter and Facebook, TikTok is able to get you fifty times more engagement than you have with Facebook. That is not a number to take lightly and it is something to really think about. If you have fifty times more engagement with followers on TikTok than Facebook use it. Use TikTok to your advantage and get those followers. It will also give you over a hundred times more engagement per follower than a Twitter account. Those numbers are huge! That is a big difference. This is why all of the big businesses and brands are jumping on TikTok and not the other social media platforms anymore. However, it is important to note that they still use them together with TikTok because they realized that there is a benefit to doing all of them together and you can amass a larger following.

It is also said that visual content is easier because it is quick and it does not take as much time as written content. Another benefit that it offers is that you can look at it without much effort at all. This is why TikTok is a hot commodity and it is a hot favorite for users around the web to use. It just takes time to get this right. When you first get on TikTok you might think that this is going to be the easiest thing you've ever done and all you have to do is snap a picture but it's more than that. You need to create the right pictures along with the need to get engagement. You also have to have ideas and reach your audience. All of these things could be a very challenging task. However, once you start doing it understanding TikTok and what you need for it will get easier and you begin to take better pictures and understand the content better as well. Just keep reminding yourself that it does get easier because you are getting used to it.

Many people ask the question of why high-quality content is so important and it is because you have to rethink your content strategy and your photos if you want to stay relevant. After all, everybody is using the TikTok now. TikTok is not meant to stop you from growing your business it's meant to help you grow it, but it definitely will compel you to rework your TikTok content strategy so that you can create the best content for TikTok and make sure that the people are still interested in what you have to say and what you have to show. You can plan your TikTok content strategy simply by asking who your audience is and what type of content you think they will want to see. Finding your audience and their likes and dislikes are going to take some time and how you can get them to want to see your page and want to see what you have to say. All you have to do is keep rolling out that content and make sure that it is the best that you can give. If you are a jewelry brand for example then you should put out photos revolving around jewelry, but you should not just take a picture of a necklace on a display. Instead, what you should do is you should make sure that it looks beautiful and that it has great lighting so that your audience will be able to see it better. Make sure that they will be able to see the embellishments on the jewelry better and that it will be a picture that entices them to your page for maximum results. You can share all different content on TikTok and if you are sharing things that revolve around your niche, you should share what your brand is and what you believe. This little backstory type of set up really lets you connect with your audience and help them to gain trust and loyalty to you. Do not be a faceless corporation. Show them what you are about and what it is that you believe in and stand for.

Post what goes on in the workplace or your brand as well? These photos let the audience connect with you behind the scenes and not just the services that you provide. This can be a really fun and innovative way to get people to step up and notice you as well as wanting to follow you and see what you are going to do next. If you are a company, you can also allow your employees to share their perspective on behalf of the brand or product, and you can share photos of people using the products that you sell for your brand or your business. A good tip for you to use is to remember to have fun being creative with your products as well and make sure that they are being photographed to the best of their ability.

You can command attention with a big idea and a big theme as well. At the end of the day, this is what people want to see and using a common theme that binds those images together is going to be the best for your profile and your page. If you are finding that you are having trouble being consistent with your postings, there are ways to help with this as well. We have stressed the importance of being able to post as consistently as possible but if you're finding that this is hard for you send your audience posts at a specific time every day and this will make it easier. Having a routine in place and a schedule is a great idea for anybody on social media or even just in your regular life. This is because a schedule can keep things simple and easier for you. For example, if you want to post in the morning, make sure that you have set up to do so, and then the rest of the day you do not have to worry about anything because you have already done it.

Chapter 9: Monetizing Tiktok

Selling Your Product/Service Via TikTok

Once you have your TikTok page up and running, it's time to start generating your audience into customers! Remember, don't hesitate to sell your service or products. You don't want to just consistently provide free value and knowledge without any return for yourself because at the end of the day, you run a business. So now it's time to think of your plan of attack towards how you can sell your products and services within your business.

Getting Started

If you don't already have a website set up, you can still promote your business just via TikTok. Posting photos, videos and Stories of your business in action or the products you sell is a good way to get your customers to trust you and want to buy. At the end of the day, if they have liked your page, they have an interest in what you offer and you will convert more customers than you think as long as you provide quality value that is authentic.

Driving TikTok Traffic to your Business

If you have a product or service, make sure the link to your website or the products are in your TikTok Bio as well as all your other social media accounts.

Posting

TikTok has many different kinds of posts, and they are always adding more to the roster. They will likely have at least one more on this list before the year is out.

Using Stories

Stories are a great feature that was recently built in to TikTok pages, as well as private pages. This feature allows you to share exclusive, behind the scenes footage of your business in action. It gives you a great advantage in getting customers excited about what you are offering, as well as allowing them to feel personally involved in what you are doing in your business. When people support your business, they want to feel important to you and your business. Brand experience is a great way to boost that. Through stories, you can share important moments that customers would otherwise miss. This can include fun things such as unboxing new products, sharing a live video during a customer session (with customer consent,) or even just sharing a short video of what you and your staff are doing on your days off. One great thing about TikTok stories is that you can actually add to them from Instagram. If you have a business Instagram account linked to your TikTok page, when you share stories with your Instagram account, you can set them to share to TikTok as well. This means that a broader audience sees your stories and that you are nurturing both platforms at the same time.

Videos

Using posts with photographs and videos is a great way to share your business with your audience. When it comes to selling specifically, you want to make sure that you are sharing high-quality images or videos of your products and services. For example, taking a high-resolution image of your product with a beautiful background in a well-lit area is a great way to make the image more attractive, thus attracting the audience to you even more. Alternatively, sharing an image of you performing a service (with customers' consent) is another great way. For example, if you are a hairdresser, you might have a co-worker take a high-quality picture of you cutting a client's hair. Then, you can share it with a caption such as, "Had so much fun cutting (customer's name)'s hair today! PS, I have a few more appointments available this weekend. Call xxx-xxx-xxxx to book!" This is a great way to show off your business through your posts and drive traffic to your business.

As you can see, selling through TikTok Is actually quite simple. You can get your customers to click on a specific link where you're selling your service, or you can drive the traffic from your social media account to your website, where you can then provide more value and sell them your products and services.

If not, you can simply tell your customers via private message if they're interested in the product or service you're willing to sell.

Remember, by this point, you would have done your customer research, and your page will be up and running, providing immense value. So, don't hesitate to sell your quality products.

Text Post

The original kind of TikTok post, and the most basic. A text post sparks engagement and gets your followers talking. Ask your followers questions about what they want from you and what you can do to make their lives easier, and this will get you some great engagement.

Live Video

Live video is exactly what it sounds like: a live video. It can be a great way to connect with your followers and give them behind the scene, looks at your company, your product, or even the personality behind the brand. Just remember, anything can happen during a live broadcast, so be sure to prepare yourself well for any problems that could take place.

Linked Content

Linking content on TikTok is a very popular and very easy way to get more engagement to your own website, or other content online. Be careful to only share content to your page that is relevant to you, and that you think your followers will want to share as well. Sharing is caring, everybody!

Pinned Post

Having a pinned post is when you pin a post at the top of the page. This is great for you if you have something that you feel like needs attention and should be the first post that your potential customers see as they click on your page. (ex. You're trying to sell tickets to a show. Your pinned post should be a review or a picture of the production.)

TikTok Affiliate Marketing

If you are new to the world of business and are looking for a great way to make money with your page, affiliate marketing may be something for you to look into. Affiliate marketing is a wonderful way to make passive income on your TikTok page simply by implementing the tools that you have learned throughout. In this case, you are going to learn how you can begin affiliate marketing so that you can make money through your TikTok page without having to sell your own products or services. You can solely rely on making income through Affiliate Marketing or you can use it as an extra income stream.

Affiliate marketing is a business model wherein the affiliate marketer (you) markets products for other businesses. This business model is one of the lowest maintenance models to exist, allowing you to build a passive income simply through having an engaged social media following. To make money using this business model, all you have to do is share products to your followers that are owned by other brands. Every time they purchase a product with your link or coupon code, you earn a commission from the company.

Creating a powerful affiliate marketing business requires you to build an engaged and loyal following on social media first. If you do not have an engaged and active following, people will not click on your link, and you simply won't make any money. As a result, it will be harder for you to get deals. This will not be a successful venture for you. However, if you take the time to build a loyal following through the regular posting advice given, you will be able to make plenty of money through this business model in relatively minimal timing.

Alternatives to affiliate marketing include direct sales and network marketing. In direct sales and network marketing, however, you are bound to a single company. In affiliate marketing, you can have as many deals with as many companies as you desire. You create termed contracts with these companies that enable you to promote their products in exchange for a commission, unlike in direct sales or network marketing, where you become an official representative of the chosen company. That being said, affiliate marketing is a lot freer and more lucrative than direct sales or network marketing, which is why I recommend it.

Finding Affiliate Marketing Deals

Getting started in affiliate marketing requires you to find deals that you can market. When you are a bigger online personality with a large number of engaged following, companies will begin to seek you out to do these deals. This is because they recognize the value of your marketing abilities and they want to take advantage of your services and access your audience through a person they trust most: you. When you get to this point, making your deals is pretty simple. However, until you are there, you need to know how to find affiliate marketing deals that will allow you to go through with them when your number of followers is smaller.

Once you have a few hundred followers, you can begin looking on websites like ClickBank or Amazon associates to receive affiliate marketing deals. These websites are based on connecting companies with marketers so that affiliate marketing deals can be made. Companies on these websites are looking for people just like you to promote them. All you have to do to get started is to create a profile, have it verified, and then begin connecting with companies who are ready to make deals with you.

When you are making your deal, make sure that you pay attention to the terms of it. You do not want to enter a deal that may be restrictive, limiting, or unfair to you. Some companies may want to make deals that do not involve cash. For example, they may give you product credit to their company in exchange for your services. This is not necessarily a bad thing, but you need to decide if it is something you are willing to accept. Knowing what you are and are not willing to accept into your deals will make it easier to finalize them or negotiate them if need be.

Lastly, do not be too hard on yourself if you have a deal that is not exactly what you expected or if things started off somewhat slow. Staying dedicated and continuing to put the effort will pay off in the end. Your commitment is your success, so keep showing up. Before you know it, you will be earning a major passive income through your affiliate marketing deals.

Another way to find affiliate marketing deals is by emailing the company and letting them know that you would be happy to sell their product through an affiliate program. They will give you a special link in which lets the company know that they are your customers who are buying their product/service. Some companies have an affiliate program you can automatically sign up to on their website also.

Posting Your Affiliate Marketing Posts

When you are posting your affiliate marketing posts, make sure that you verify the terms of your agreement with the company you are promoting for. Additionally, verify the terms of the agreement with the site you are sharing it on, and any legal requirements you may have. For example, recently, a law was passed stating that if you are using affiliate links in a blog post, you must post a disclaimer at the top of your post to let people know that you are being paid for promoting the company with your link.

Keeping yourself protected by knowing what is expected of you is the best way to ensure that a good deal does not go sour accidentally. If you want to remain professional, stay in business, keep your accounts active, and avoid potential lawsuits, staying protected by doing what is legally required of you is essential.

Aside from paying attention to your legal obligations, posting for your promotional posts with affiliate links is simple. These pointers will still apply as they are the best tools that you can use to promote on TikTok. If you are permitted to by the company, you may also consider boosting the post to increase visibility and maximize the amount of money you make through that link. Always be sure to ask first, however, as not all companies will be okay with you promoting their links through paid advertising.

Remember, if you're going to sell an affiliate product, make sure it relates to your business, and it is something that you truly believe will benefit your customers. Quality and personal benefit are the main factors you want to consider when selling any type of product. And losing your customers' trust can highly affect your business. Remember, you are a quality provider only!

TikTok Shop

Well, nowadays, TikTok isn't just a place for marketing your product anymore. Now you can actually sell the product right on TikTok. Yes, you read that. TikTok now lets you have the ability to create a TikTok shop page and directly sell items to your followers.

This is another feature that is very, very new, and not very many people are taking advantage of it.

Your first thought might be "no way" but stop and think about it. TikTok is the most popular website in the world, and average users spend about 20 minutes per day on the platform. That adds up to over two hours every week. That's a lot of time.

It's also not that hard to believe, considering our own experiences with social media. We've all fallen down the rabbit hole, haven't we? Where we spend at least an hour scrolling through our feed, tapping links, and liking posts?

There's no harm in taking advantage of TikTok as a social media platform, so there's certainly no harm in using it as a selling platform. It's not a fully evolved one, with all the bells and whistles, like Etsy or eBay, but it does its job.

To do this, you're first going to need a TikTok business page. On your page, Locate the shop tab to the left and click on it. You're going to have to give TikTok information, such as your tax number and your address. For payment, you can link your bank account.

After this is all done, you're ready to go! You can add a product to your shop/s.

People may see TikTok as an odd place to sell things, at least directly, but think of it's this way: you're making the time they have to wait to pay shorter, meaning they have a small window to change their mind.

Chapter 10: Creating an Effective Marketing Strategy

Pages very rarely become popular by accident. You might hear the one in a million stories about the person who posted a picture online, and it blew up and made them famous instantly, but, more than likely, your popular pages started with a plan of action. Just posting information on your social media isn't going to draw people to your page. In order to gain followers, you have to provide content that they want to look at. People on TikTok are looking through posts after posts as they scroll through their feed of followers. If they go to the search homepage, they see randomly generated photos that they may find interesting based on what they have liked in the past and currently follow. This is because an algorithm notices when you look at something for a longer period of time than you spend on other posts. When you look at something for an extended period of time, the TikTok algorithm studies that topic and pushes out more information related to that in order to keep your attention on their platform for longer. Social media sites are not making money if you aren't using the platform. Companies are paying them to advertise their content to users in order to build up their reputation in the process. The longer you look at something, the more advertisements get thrown on the feed, which creates more profit for the advertising company and the social media platform itself. That's why you need to know how to use the algorithm to your advantage when you begin posting regularly online and communicating with your followers.

On the TikTok search page, you'll notice a few different things: the search bar at the top, the clickable category choices, and the photos and videos on display. You have the choice to look through the photos selected for you based on what you've liked and the different profiles you follow, or you can click on a topic bar at the top and look through the photos that appear under that specific topic. If you're looking for a specific hashtag, you can always type that into the search bar as well in order to find pictures with that same label. People usually search for general hashtags, which is why it's a good idea to have different categories of tags on your post to increase the likelihood that someone will come across it and look at it.

There are several ways to draw the attention of viewers in order to get them to follow your page or like a photo that you posted. There are a lot of techniques that will help you get to the base you want, and they also help you sell your product. Let's say you're trying to raise money for a charity event, and you want to get more people than just your followers involved. You have to come up with a way to spread the word while maintaining the hype. You could make a contest to get the word spread from person to person by having people compete by tagging one another online. You could also ask followers to donate a dollar for a special promotional rate. Whatever it is you are trying to achieve online, developing a strategy is your first step.

The Posting Algorithm

The posting algorithm is a mathematical magic formula in a computer that recognizes how popular posts are and who likes them based on how many times they have been looked at and how long someone looks at them. The more that people look at a post about a certain topic, the more likely it is that the algorithm will put more of that content in their news feeds for them to view. It gives TikTok the views and time that they want on their platform while the person gets new posts to view on a favorite topic.

The main idea of any social media site is to post relevant content for your followers consistently. If you are not posting consistently and the information is not updated, people might lose interest in your page. Each post is accounted for in the TikTok algorithm, which means that the more you post, the more likely people are to see that content. If someone spends a longer period of time looking at one post over the others, then the algorithm likes it more and deems it more credible than other posts. The more credible your posts are, the more likely it is that your company's posts will appear at the top of the content.

Think about it like this, if you post a team office photo and everyone in that photo likes it, the algorithm will note the popularity and extend it to your next post as well, under the assumption that it will have the same popularity levels. The more posts you make, the more the algorithm can average out the popularity. While not all posts will get hundreds of likes, you can attempt to make them as compelling as possible by running a contest or running promotions for liked content.

The algorithm, in particular, is looking for people to stay on and use TikTok. The longer they are looking at their feed online, the more opportunities it creates to show them advertisements for products and companies, which is how TikTok makes its money. So, if your posts are capable of capturing peoples' attention for an extended period of time, then TikTok is going to reward that by pushing it higher in the algorithm of what posts are seen.

How do you make the algorithm work in your favor? There are several ways to get your information to the top of your followers' feed. While TikTok was originally designed for users to post photos, videos began gaining popularity as well. The TikTok algorithm does not prioritize videos unless the audience looking at them does. This means, if your followers don't take the time to stop and watch a video in their feed, the system isn't going to continue to push more videos to the top. It is only going to prioritize what the user is looking at most frequently (Cooper, 2019). Take videos into consideration by determining how long your followers are looking at them. While you don't want to have long drawn out videos, thirty seconds to a minute will hold their attention. Then, the algorithm notices them staying longer on your page and looking at your posts, pushing you further up on the viewing scale.

You also need to consider when to post. People aren't constantly looking at social media, but there are key times when people scroll through their feeds that should be noted. Depending on your audience, you may need to post in the early morning or late at night when you aren't awake. You can use planners like TikTok Scheduler or Hootsuite, which allow you to schedule posts for certain times and then automatically put them out when the system sends a signal. Using a scheduler also allows you the ability to plan posts in advance and schedule them to post at a later date. For example, if you are having a large company event and the flyers have already been made, you can take a photo of the flyer and schedule it to post a few days in advance of the event, along with other information released on the day of the event itself. You can even create a post with your event hashtag on it and set it up to release on the day of the event. This way, you don't have to worry about posting while everything else is being planned.

Another key aspect to take advantage of is simply asking people to turn on their notifications for your company's posts. When you think about it logically, the notification setting is probably one of the easiest ways to get your followers to look at your posts. When a notification pops up on your phone, you automatically go to see what it's about. Now that phones give you the ability to just click on the notification and follow it to the link or page, people have more ease of access to their social media and messages and can look at them just as quickly as the notification that pops up.

Running a contest on TikTok is also a great way to boost yourself up in the algorithm. Usually, contests consist of tagging people in the post or following and posting something with a company hashtag attached. This creates an influx of followers and comments on posts that make your posts seem more popular in the system. While running contests is a quick way to boost your score in the system, it does average out, and you have to make sure that you keep your posting up to keep the algorithm from pushing you back down the ladder.

Overall, the algorithm breaks down into three categories: content, consistency, and attention. The more consistently you post, the more likely people will see your page and begin following you. The content needs to be well-timed, and the message should be delivered using descriptive hashtags from different categories. Both of those combined get you the attention you need in order for people to view, like, and comment on your posts and photos. This may convert visitors into followers who can constantly see the content that you post.

Using Effective Photography

Photography has a lot to do with how a product is marketed. Several factors go into taking a photo post-worthy and attention-grabbing. You don't need to have a fancy camera or a professional photographer to take a good photo. While it can be helpful to have someone take the photo for you, selfie pictures and candid moments can be some of the most emotion-filled photos because they represent the people behind the camera and what they are trying to voice for the company.

Good photography can make all the difference when it comes to people viewing your online profile. If the picture quality of your posts is consistently bad, then it will shed a bad light on the capabilities of a business. As ridiculous as it may seem, people are comparing the quality of your social media page to the work they believe that you can do for them. If you work for a marketing company and your TikTok page is just a host of blurry photos and non-descriptive posts, then customers might be less likely to trust your capability when it comes to producing clear and effective marketing projects.

A study done by Curalate in 2013 compiled four different aspects that affected the popularity of a photo (Gotter, 2019):

- *Use Lighter Images* — While this may seem a little self-explanatory, having the correct lighting and colors in a photo can make a difference. No one wants to struggle to see the details of a photo. The details should be noticeable and bold to the eye.
- *More Background or White Space Is Preferred* — You don't want too much going on in a photo. If you are trying to sell a new boat, you shouldn't have a picture filled with different boats and yours in the middle. More than likely, you'll have the boat you are advertising on a plain or simple background so

that the person's eye is drawn directly to the object that you are promoting.

- *Dominance Matters* — Just like having one item in the picture, it's best not to go color crazy. The study showed that if the more dominant color was blue rather than red, the photo produced more likes. This also held true for photos that only had one dominant color instead of many.
- *Use Contrasting Textures* — Having too many textures going on in your picture can be overwhelming, but having one or two to contrast with your dominant texture does bring attention to the photo.

TikTok Contest 101

A TikTok contest is one of the best ways to boost your following and get people to look at your page. It also gets people to come back and check for new information about the contest or results that they are waiting for. As we have previously established, the more that people look at your page, the more the algorithm likes your TikTok account. In order to run a successful contest on any platform, there are several steps you need to take before people start entering. While some legal steps have to be taken with a contest, we are only going to go over the basics of how to set the contest up and move it in the correct direction. You should discuss legal matters of the topic with your company lawyer.

- *Contest Goal* — The first big step to planning any contest is figuring out your goal. Your goal isn't just to give away free stuff to internet strangers, so what exactly are you trying to achieve? Do you want to get more followers for your page? Are you just trying to get more likes and comments on some of your photos? Maybe you're trying to gauge the customer's reaction to certain products or styles of work by having them vote on their favorites. Whatever you are trying to achieve needs to be your main goal, and you should write it down for data comparison later.

- *Entry Method* — Next, you need to come up with the entry method. How do you want people to enter and participate in the contest? Do they need to like the photo and tag three friends? Do they need to post a separate picture with a particular hashtag for competition? Maybe they need to take a quick survey to be entered into the competition. However, you plan to go about having people enter, make sure the instructions are clear. You should also develop a hashtag for the contest. Even if it's not necessary for people to create a new post with the hashtag, you want something that people can click on and follow so that they can enter the contest as well. If you have people share the post as one of the requirements for the contest, it helps spread the word to different types of people and also helps your page as far as the algorithm is concerned.

- *Contest Theme* — You also need to have a theme for the contest. Maybe it's wintertime and you're running a contest to win new skis and a trip to the mountains. For obvious reasons, you would want to come up with something clever and catchy that relates the product to the competition. You could say something like #meanttoski and use it around Valentine's Day as a play on the phrase "meant to be." You are tying in the theme of falling in love with the new skis and the trip you are promoting. The idea for all themes remains the same. You want the theme to be clever but simple enough for people to remember it and share it with their friends and family.

- *Pick a Winner* — Lastly, you have to decide when the cutoff date for the contest is and how to determine the winner. There are three ways to pick a winner: random selection, selected jury, and popular vote. Random selection is a great way to pick from a large number of people. If all you asked them to do was like and follow your page, then it is easy enough to run their names through a random generator for a completely fair way to pick a winner. If you choose to have a jury judge the competition, then it involves a little more work. You'll need to bring in extra professionals to judge the submissions from all the competitors. While this is fair and is based on the quality of work rather than the randomness of a like and follow, it does take more time and attention to detail on the company's part. Finally, you have the voting method, which is simply having people vote to pick a winner. While this is a good way to get contestants motivated and followers involved, the scales can be tipped occasionally. If you have one contestant that has 10 followers while another has 10.5 million, the ability for that contestant to share their request for votes is higher than the others. Is that necessarily a problem? No, but it does make it more of a popularity contest than a true competition. You can always use a mix of these methods as well. You could have judges narrow the contestants down to five and then allow followers to vote and pick their favorites. While there can still be a little bit of unfairness to the plan, it does narrow down the finalists to the people who actually successfully completed the competition.

After you are finished designing and finalizing all the contest work, you just have to promote it. Put the hashtag out there and advertise the contest on your different forms of social media for the company. Let people share it and spread the word as much as possible to get people motivated to join and participate in your company's main page.

When you go to announce the winner of the contest, make sure to thank people for participating. Again, it's all about the interaction you have on TikTok. You can also post when you are holding another contest in order to keep people returning to your page to stay up to date with any promotion your company may be running.

Chapter 11: Marketing Mistakes to Avoid on Tiktok

Simply having a business page on TikTok does not guarantee that your ad campaign will succeed. Everyone is prone to make mistakes. Although mistakes are not always bad, especially if you can learn from them. However, it is a great idea always to stay clear of the mistakes rather than wasting time and energy.

Using a profile to promote your business

Oftentimes people avoid the hassle and promote their business using a TikTok profile. It is not recommended. If you do so, you will not be able to analyze the results. TikTok profiles do not use any tracking tools; hence all the efforts will go to waste. Without the analytics and engagement status in your information toolbox, you will not be able to develop the right strategy.

Secondly, sending a friend request as a business is considered creepy. This is different compared to like a page. When you send a friend request, it is just like asking the user to share personal data. It is a violation of social boundaries. Lastly, it is also against the TikTok's Terms of

Service. What's the point of investing resources when the profile will be deleted anyway?

Posting at a bad times

This is an important element to consider when it comes to TikTok marketing. A lot of marketers tend to overlook this aspect. They forget that majority of the buyers have a 9-5 job and will not be logging in at that time. Posting in the period of the workday is usually not effective compared to putting up a post in the early evening or even morning.

When brand's post at a user's presence, then it increases the likelihood of reaching out. You can easily schedule posts using Post Planner.

Optimizing Ads Too Often

The majority of the advertisers on TikTok consistently turn up the knobs of the ads believing that altering the budget, bids and the targets will lead to quicker progress. In reality, optimization resets the ad rank and positions it at the start of the learning stage.

Similarly, having more does not automatically increase your chances of winning. Every ad set must reach at least 50 conversations weekly. If you waste the budget on multiple ads, then you will not have one strong ad to reach the goal. You will have to depend on bigger audience pools and lookalike audiences. Find your winners using a 3 step funnel of awareness, consideration, and conversion. Then invest in that.

Don't advertise through a group

Some of the marketers try to advertise through a variety of groups. This is a common mistake and is not very effective. Groups on TikTok are created to facilitate individuals to connect with one another based on similar interests or goals. Concentrating the efforts on a single brand is difficult. A group is successful when all the members have an equal role. Groups with a solitary entity directing topics usually aren't effective.

Overzealous or Insensitive Posting

In the enthusiastic marketing plans, businesses forget about the value that the ads offer to the followers. Studies suggest that clogging a customer's newsfeed has led to a fall of many companies, and the same can happen to you. Excessively adding posts several times in a day will only lead to avoidance and might even result in your page being reported.

To protect people, TikTok has designed an algorithm that ensures that they do not get to see extra posts. It shows that high volume posting will only push the clientele away.

Users might even unlike the page, and it will be impossible to get them back. Going more than 5 posts a day is overkill.

Don't ignore comments

TikTok fans are individuals, just like you. When they leave a comment on your business page, they automatically expect a preceding comment or reply. This is an indication that you are listening. Brand pages that constantly overlook comments by fans do not succeed. It is because fans won't return to the page if they feel unheard. Secondly, when you respond, the client automatically revisits the page.

Not Having Enough Visuals

All of us love viewing images rather than text. Similarly, our customers would like the same. Reading long posts is exhausting. This is why brands need to ensure that their posts are short and to the point. The best way to draw attention is with captivating visuals, combined with text that exemplifies your point. Concentrate on giving top-notch pictures and save the marketing terminology to a minimum.

Having a Relaxed Approach

Marketers indulge in another common mistake by taking their page lightly, similar to how they treat their profiles.

Individuals that utilize TikTok profiles seldom have the main business agenda. For the most part, using profiles on TikTok is a totally different activity that is fun. You must have a well thought out strategy that integrates understanding your fan base, offering a special message, and computing results.

Copy and Pasting Competitor's Strategy

Some TikTok marketers are lazy to the point where they would look at their competitors and simply imitate the ad structure. Even if they make slight alterations, chances are they will end up failing. Wondering why that is? It is because your rival will initially expend a huge amount of resources to optimize their marketing efforts. However, copying them won't give you a competitive advantage.

Behind the scenes and analysis behind a strategy is as important as the ad itself. When you copy the ad, you will not be aware of what you are doing right. You may not be aware of the segment that delivers results. It is quite possible that you say the wrong things at the right time or you may even address the right people with the wrong stuff —result: failure.

Being too pushy or selling it too little

Selling too much is perhaps the most widely made a mistake by businesses who promote on TikTok. Let's suppose you set up a page and instantly begin posting content that revolves around your services or products. This will not work because users are not concerned with the products. All they worry about are the things associated with those products or services. For instance, if you are a sports shop, then instead of advertising your products, you can discuss hiking places and embed the store link.

On the contrary, selling too little is a possible mistake. Let's take the above example a little further. If the sports store learned about selling too much and stop selling too much, but even then, the sales do not increase. This is because TikTok users enjoy conversing.

Quitting Paid Marketing Too Early

The majority of the marketers have a one-time mindset, which means that they will spend but only once. They might pull out their investment quickly if the campaign results are not what they expected. It might even lead them to quit TikTok altogether. Just because one campaign is not successful, it does not mean that you pull the plug. Rather you can stop the campaign and initiate a new one.

Avoid these mistakes to ensure that you utilize the investment in the best manner.

Conclusion

To reach your target audience, you have to know who they are. And to know who they are, you have to think about their age, their location, their relationship status, their agenda, the personality, their interest, their education, and their career. You need to ask yourself what do your audience want and how you will give it to them. You need to ask yourself what they need and if you can provide that thing. You need to ask yourself which problem they have and if you can solve that problem. You need to ask yourself what their dreams are, and can you help them to achieve those dreams. How will they be entertained, and can you entertain them? Most importantly, how are they going to follow you? You need to know what your target audience's biggest motivations are.

The biggest shift in moving from having a typical account to having an account that will generate revenue from for you is to shift your perspective from being self-centered to being audience-centered. First of all, you need to answer these above questions even though you will realize some of the questions require more specific answers than others. For instance, you might not want to target only one gender, but at least you have thought about it, and you have explained why you don't want to target only one gender.

The point of all this is for you to be as intentional as possible about your target audience. You need to ask yourself constantly, why don't I know my target audience. If you don't know your target audience, then you need to think Deeply. You can create some imaginary people that you think would be your perfect followers. Give them some backstories. Give them a hair color. Give them names. Give them different names. Have a solid visual perception of the people that you are creating your content for. You might even find out that your target audience is very similar to you. If that's what you found out, then that is great because you already know yourself better than everyone else. You need to think about all your dreams and visions and all the answers to the questions that you mentioned above. And how to target your target audience.

You should think about the TikTok account that you enjoy looking at the most and ask yourself what do I like about this TikTok account and why do I even like it in the first place? Why or ask yourself why don't I like this account in the first place or why does it bother me?

If you don't know any TikTok account that you enjoy him, then you should go to your niche and look at all the TikTok account that you follow and write down all your thoughts and opinions about the TikTok account.

Go where they are

Now once you have nowhere, your target audience has been. You should go where they're hanging. They are already hanging out somewhere. Your mission is to find those pages that they are following. Find the TikTok accounts that they like. Find those topics that they are commenting on. Find out where they are. Find their favorite pasta. Find out their favorite account. Find out their favorite TikTok account. And then start following them. Start building a relationship with those accounts. Get to know their hashtags, the hashtags are usually the best place to start looking around those pages, and you find the accounts that are already big players there.

Organize your marketing goes

Once you have decided to work on TikTok, then you have already switched into the world of marketing. And all you need to do to go is to change your thought process and start thinking like a marketer. Do you know that you are already officially a brand once you create a TikTok account so every decision that you make needs to be in line with this brand? Brands have their rules, algorithms, and regulations, so you need to have your own rules and regulations.

TikTok rules are always changing, they are never permanent, and it can make life difficult for you. But your goal is to change no matter what TikTok throws at you. The basis of marketing will always remain the same, and the basic principle of effective marketing is for you to go where they already are. Know what you want them to do and know who you want to reach. And you need to know what you want to do with them. You need to allow them to understand what is in for them and what will be easy to make them act.

You need to be patient and flexible with them. You got to know that no two accounts at the same, even if they look very similar. This means what will work brilliantly for one account will not work for another account, even if you create 11 different accounts that are nearly identical in the same industry. You're targeting the same audience and using the same voice to target all the audience.

You still cannot use one strategy for all account, because the same thing will not work for different accounts. There are many TikTok experts out there telling you to use one certain strategy, but you have to understand that one strategy will not work for all. Even if you get progress today, it doesn't mean that you will get progress tomorrow, because things might change. Even if you copy the strategies that big account uses, it might not work for you.

You might read a strategy that somebody used to gain 20 followers in 5 minutes, but when you try the strategy, you might only get one follower in 5 minutes, and that will unfollow you shortly after. Then after some months again, you might try that strategy, and it will work. After some time, you will discover that all your old tricks are no longer working, so you will have nothing else to do. So, you should never get too comfortable with TikTok, you have to be changing, and you have to be trying things out and testing things out simple ideas and don't expect anyone to work for the long-term.

Just constantly watch your results and keep on brainstorming new ideas or new approaches.

Determine your vision

You need to ask yourself questions about your product and your brand. If you are marketing a product to your followers that you haven't released yet, then you can ask one of your followers to test that product out. For instance, if you are marketing a seasonal product from Starbucks, you can also use it as if they are excited to be part of it. Asking your followers to comment on their favorite post or product is a great way to encourage engagement with them and to market your product. But it will also encourage them to leave positive comments rather than negative ones.

You could simply ask your followers simple questions like what you will wear with those blue shoes. So, try to create a vision for your TikTok account to determine what you want to be over time. And what you want your account today and exactly what you want your account to say. The time in which you want to post in the morning, and exactly what you want to post in the night and determine who your account is going to help, and who your account is not going to help. So that you won't once people come to your account, they will already know if the account is for them or if the account is not for them.

They cannot instantly know if they should follow you or if they should not follow you. If you check your current TikTok account or any of your social media accounts, I'm sure you will see tons of people that are not your target market following you. You will see people that can't even speak your language following you, and this is bad for business. If you are trying to build a TikTok page that is able to generate money for you, then you need to be able to specify a target audience. You don't need a general target audience for your TikTok account, you need a very specific audience .you need specific people who are coming to look for specific kind of results to follow you, you don't want just any random person to follow you.

If you are building a TikTok account that sells clothes, then you need people who are interested in fashion to follow you. If you are building a TikTok account that sells shoes, then you need to sell to high-class ladies that are interested in shoes to follow you. The same thing, if you are selling watches on your TikTok account, then you need people that are interested in luxury things to follow you. If you are trying to sell high fashionable clothes or a 2020 model type of clothes, then you wouldn't want somebody that is 60 years old to be following you. The same thing applies, if you are sending women shoes, you wouldn't want men to be following your TikTok account.

You will only want women to be following your TikTok account. So, you have to determine your vision for your TikTok account. You also need to determine where this account will be in the following 5 years. Are you going to sell it off? Are you going to start an affiliate marketing? Are you going to start dropshipping products? Are you going to sell digital products? What exactly do you intend to do with the TikTok account?

You have to determine all that upfront, even before you create the TikTok account, even before you click on the sign-in button on TikTok; you have to determine exactly where your account is going to lead to. If you intend to sell affiliate products on your TikTok account, you will manage it differently than if you want to drop ship products on your TikTok account, and you will manage it differently if you want to sell digital products on your TikTok account. Also, you need to determine which name is going to be using. You need to determine all of this upfront.

Direct users to click your profile

Even if you're utilizing the clickable link in your bio, you have to update it to the current all relevant content and make your users know that you have updated the link in your caption. You could say something like, want to learn more about this link, then click on my bio. This is great especially when you're posting the video or a photograph of a product, and you want users to be able to engage with the product and buy from you. You could also put a shopper bill link in your bio and write something like, "to shop this product, then follow the link in our bio." Try to offer additional insights to the link or supporting data. This is no brainer, and especially the caption is the best place to capture your followers and provide them with more information on the content of the photograph or the video or to provide them with unique insight or supporting data that they may not have known before.

You could also post the photo of a member of your team or an industry leader, and when you post their photography, you also want to include the names of the people in the caption and provide more information about those people. You could also post their achievements, and who they are.

Encourage action

If the image that you are posting features a particular product, then try to encourage the users to purchase the product by telling them to get their hands on it. And then provide additional information to the link of the website that you want them to purchase it, and also the price of the product that you want them to purchase. You should also encourage them to take action by donating if you are a non-profit company, or you could also post the link for them to attend a brand-related event. To do that, you just need to post the image of the shot or the venue, the image of the setting, and say something like, "join us today at 2.pm time, for more important connections, interesting conversations, and great refreshments." Always use fill in the blank sentences.

A great way to encourage engagement with your post and your followers is to offer them insights and fill in the blank statements by saying something like, "my favorite way to start the day is blank, and then use the photograph of somebody that is enjoying your product in the morning, that way, followers will be able to state their own personal routines under the comments section, and this will make your followers be able to associate your product with their morning routine without you even being aggressive or too forward about it.

Made in the USA
Monee, IL
07 April 2022

94295739R00085